Justa
Happy Cook

A Chef's Life

Farm-to-Table Cooking
in the Berkshires

By Michael Ballon

Contents

Food Trends

Profiles in Farming

Running a Restaurant

In Memoriam

Acknowledgements

My thanks to the many loyal and regular customers who have supported us over the years, a dedicated and hard-working staff who have given their blood, sweat, and tears, and the ever-growing number of farmers and food artisans who help make creating good food possible.

I am indebted to Caroline Alexander and *Berkshire-foodjournal.com*, who generously contributed the portraits of Berkshire farms and farmers.

Thanks also to *Homestyle Magazine*, where many of these essays first appeared.

To Karin, who spent almost as much time with this book as I did, and who knows all too well the challenges of life with a chef.

Foreword

TWENTY-FIVE YEARS AGO, when the Castle Street Café was newly opened, my wife and I ate our first dinner there. We were astounded. We had not eaten such a delicious and innovative meal at any other restaurant in the Berkshires, let alone in Great Barrington. Indeed, the only other restaurants at which we had dined so well were located in major cities.

Since that time, Great Barrington has emerged as the centre gastronomique for all of Western Massachusetts. This quiet New England town of 7,000 has become our region's Dijon, boasting, at last count, a good three chefs of the first rank. I have no doubt that Michael Ballon's Castle Street Café marked the beginning of this happy development.

Recently, Ballon has again been in the vanguard by creating a gourmet menu of locally raised meats and vegetables. So it is no surprise that some of the most captivating essays in this volume are found in the section 'Profiles in Farming'. This veteran chef has figured out how to fashion delectable dishes out of indigenous ingredients. 'Home grown' plus 'healthy' need not add up to 'bland' after all.

Another section of this book that I thoroughly enjoyed was titled 'Running a Restaurant'. Like many people I know, I have had a recurring fantasy of running my own restaurant. After reading this section, I am reconsidering this fantasy: it still sounds like great fun, but who has the energy for all the multi-tasking needed to make a first rate restaurant run smoothly?

Ballon has generously seasoned this food memoir with wit. One section is titled 'Evolution of a Dish, or 6 Degrees of Kevin Bacon'; it is about a chicken dish that, resulting from a visit by a movie star, became eponymously wrapped. Another section is called 'A Latke Went to Indonesia'. Yes, instead of a temperamental celebrity chef in the kitchen, what we've got here is a jester in a toque.

What Ballon has also given us are recipes galore. Thank you, Mike, though even equipped with these recipes I cannot begin to approximate what comes out of your kitchen. I am afraid it's a little like a magician showing me the secrets behind his tricks: I still won't be able to fool anybody who is paying close attention. My guests and I would be far better off dropping by the Castle Street Café for the real magic.

— *Daniel Klein*

PART I

Being a Chef

. . . .

Blueberries and the Beginnings of a Chef

MANY CHEFS can pinpoint the moment in their lives when they knew they would have a career in food. For the great French chef and cookbook author Jacques Pépin that came early. His family ran a hotel and restaurant, and while quite young, he was sent off to begin training under the old apprentice system. At the time, the lowest position in the kitchen was not dishwasher or potato peeler. Instead, it was the person who stoked the ovens with coal for an hour or two early in the morning, so the ovens would be hot enough to cook. Thus began a career that led to cooking for the French president.

As Ruth Reichl recounts in her memoir *Tender at the Bone*, the *Gourmet* magazine editor began to cook because of her family. To compensate for her mother's mental illness, she would check the family meal to make sure it was edible. Reichl learned she had to examine the contents of the refrigerator to make sure her mother wasn't using spoiled ingredients. Her mother's illness meant that her cooking might sicken the family, so Reichl took the task upon herself. Years later, she found herself in the heart of the California food revolution, cooking at some of the hottest restaurants.

Julia Child had never been exposed to great French cooking until going abroad. When she joined her husband in Paris after the war, she fell in love with the cuisine; the food was like nothing she had grown up eating or cooking. At the time, women were relatively uncommon students at the French Cordon Bleu cooking school. After taking a few classes, however, she was determined to pursue her love of food further and spread the gospel of French cuisine. She would become one of the most widely known cooks around the world.

Looking back, I can identify my own "aha" moment during the summer after my sophomore year of college. I grew up with a mother who was a great cook, and in a family that prized old fashioned, homemade food, but I never thought it would be a career for me. I was going to be a lawyer. That summer I went to Bar Harbor, Maine, and got a job in a fast food fried seafood restaurant just outside Acadia National Park. But it wasn't the restaurant job that piqued my interest. No, it was the abundance of wild blueberries that grew all over the

National Park, and that were yours, free for the picking. My mother made a great blueberry pie, and my father's birthday was unthinkable without one, but I had never made one myself. That summer, I took up pie making in earnest, and even threw a blueberry pie/bring your own ice cream party for friends. In a letter home at the end of the summer, and that my mother saved, I announced, "This is to inform you that you are no longer the premier blueberry pie maker in the country. You must now share that title with me." I'm not sure I knew it then, but in retrospect it was one of the defining moments in my career. There may have been an even earlier indication of my interests, however. According to my mother, the first book I ever checked out from the public library was titled *The Blueberry Pie Elf*. It was about an elf who falls into a blueberry pie and discovers that the only escape is to eat his way out.

Blueberries are not quite as abundant in the Berkshires as they are in Maine, but throughout the region there are a lot of places where you can pick wild berries. Yes, you can go to the store and buy them, but there is nothing as satisfying as picking your own. In an age when many of us can scarcely unglue ourselves from computer screens, foraging through dense brush to pick wild berries is a great way to reconnect with our essential animal nature. Don't forget to bring along a pack on your next hike. Many times I have forgotten one, only to return from a hike with my shirt pockets bulging with berries.

Making pie dough for a traditional pie is an intimidating kitchen task for many people, but I have discovered an easier way to make a satisfying blueberry dessert. Handling pie dough is tricky, and rolling it out makes a bit of a mess, but making this cobbler recipe is simple and within the grasp of even a beginner.

Blueberry Cobbler (Serves 6-8)

Ingredients

Filling	Topping
3 pints blueberries	¾ cup sugar
1¼ cup sugar	1 cup flour
¾ cup cold water	1 tsp. baking powder
3 t cornstarch	1 egg
Dash cinnamon	3 t melted butter
Dash nutmeg	
Grated zest of 1 lemon	

Directions

1. Preheat the oven to 350 degrees Fahrenheit.

2. Combine 2 pints of blueberries with the sugar, cold water, cornstarch, spices and lemon zest into a saucepot. Bring to a boil, stirring constantly. The cornstarch will thicken the mix.

3. Puree the cooked berry mix briefly on "pulse" in a food processor.

4. In a mixing bowl, combine the cooked berries with the remaining pint of raw berries, and mix well.

5. Pour the berry mix into individual ramekins, or into a shallow baking dish.

6. To make the topping, combine the sugar, flour and baking powder in a mixing bowl, and mix in the egg. Stir well.

7. Loosely sprinkle the topping over the top of the berries, and then drizzle the melted butter on top.

8. Bake for 15 minutes in the preheated oven, and serve warm with vanilla ice cream.

Celebrity Chefs and Empires

IN JUST ONE GENERATION there has been an enormous change in the status of chefs in popular culture. In the early 60's, even among those New Yorkers who frequently ate out in the best restaurants, very few would have known or even cared about the chef's name. In the heyday of the old Classic French restaurants like Le Pavillon, it was the owner who was frequently the maître d', whose name was known. Those toiling and sweating in the back were of little interest.

The emergence of nouvelle cuisine and chef owned restaurants changed all that. In the Post War period, many of those who opened new restaurants tended to be those who had experience in the front of the house, and who aspired to own their own establishment. But as chefs began to become more prominent, they began opening their own restaurants, and instead of being relegated to the back, many designed open kitchens, with the star in full view. Instead of repeating the old tried and true classics, innovation and change became the hallmark of cuisine, and the importance of the chef started to eclipse that of the owner.

What a difference a generation makes. Superstar celebrity chefs are not only as well known as Hollywood celebrities, they are Hollywood celebrities in their own right. With their own TV shows, it's hard to keep track of all of them on the various cable channels. Anthony Bourdain, Gordon Ramsey, Tom Collichio, and Emeril Lagasse are just a few of the star chefs who have parlayed a cooking career into one primarily on television.

In this global age, the top superstar chefs now have empires stretching from both coasts of this country, with a now-obligatory outpost in Las Vegas. We are now on a first name basis with many of these star chefs, like Nobu, Mario, Daniel, and Jean-Georges. As the size of the empire increases, this top tier of chefs spends increasingly more time in television studios and flying to distant locations, rather than cooking in their own kitchens. The lure of big hotel deals and casino contracts is too tempting to resist. As the empires grow bigger and the number of restaurants these chefs own increases, so too does the cost of dining, with $300 per person meals no longer unusual.

As *New York Times* columnist Mark Bittman pointed out, those who flock to the satellite operations of some of these star chefs may find that the meal is a poor imitation of the original. When we pay top dollar to go to Fenway Park or Yankee Stadium, we want to see the real stars play, not the farm team. Yet in many of these eponymous restaurants, our meals are cooked by those trained by the Big Name rather than the chefs themselves.

Because they must train employees and supervise operations spread all over the globe, it's tough for globe-trotting chefs to cultivate and develop relationships with small farmers and local food producers. They simply aren't in one place long enough for that to happen. This is more like plane-to-table cuisine, rather than farm-to-table.

There was a time not too long ago when gastronomes would make pilgrimages to Lyon, France, dine at Paul Bocuse's or go to Roanne for the cuisine of the Troisgros brothers. These chefs spent virtually all of their working lives rooted in one place, perfecting a cuisine reflecting the region they lived in. Today you can dine in the restaurants of superstar chefs in many of the major cities

of the world, for the convenience of the international travelling business class.

The competition is fierce to see who has the most restaurants. Mario Batali now runs seven restaurants in New York, and is in the process of opening two more in Las Vegas, and one in Los Angeles. Even further apart, Alain Ducasse, with nine Michelin stars, is spread out between Monaco, Paris, New York and Las Vegas. Daniel Boulud had 13 restaurants at one point, including in Beijing, Singapore, London, Toronto, and of course New York.

In an earlier era, many great French restaurants were not located in Paris, but rather in the countryside where the chefs grew up, close to the source of the ingredients that made their food so delicious. The desire to be closer to the farms that supply their restaurants is one of the impulses behind the migration of many chefs,

including me, from New York City to the Hudson Valley and Berkshires. These chefs not only prominently feature the names of the local farms displayed on the menu, but also are actively involved in relationships with farmers.

There are no outposts of superstar chefs in the Berkshires. Instead, there is an unusual number of chef-owned restaurants, where on a daily basis working chefs filet fish, make sauces, and cook the food you eat. Many of us are on a first name basis and communicate regularly with a variety of the small farmers who supply our product. The work requires long days in hot kitchens, and is a physically demanding job, chosen because of a passion for the art, rather than for the prospect of glamorous deals or television appearances. On any given night, you can be fairly certain that the chef has actually prepared your meal.

Community Supper

A S A CATERER, most of the times I get asked to prepare food it is for festive occasions like weddings and big birthdays. Because of our location in the Berkshires, I also cater a lot of gala dinners and fundraisers for major arts and cultural organizations. Both of these types of events generally have large budgets befitting a special occasion, and there are sophisti- cated menus that go along with them.

It is therefore quite a change of pace to serve dinner for the weekly Monday night Community Supper held at the local Community Center once or twice a year. Supper is served from 5 to 6, and no reservations are required. The meal is open to the public with no questions asked, and attracts a diverse group of people.

Some are clearly there because they are experiencing financial hardship or food insecurity, and they are in need of a warm dinner. A larger number are seniors or others living alone, who seek company and camaraderie as well as a meal. There are families with young kids as well as a substantial number of elderly. The Community Center subsidizes the cost of the meal, and about 75 to 100 people show up each week.

The Center's budget is between $2.00 and $2.50 per person, which normally would barely cover the cost of a single hors d'oeuvre at a wedding or gala dinner. The challenge to me as a caterer is to provide a satisfying, balanced, and nutritious meal for that price. Some of the mainstays like filet mignon and salmon, frequently part of larger events, are not even remotely within the budget.

I am keenly aware that most of the people dining at the center rarely eat out in restaurants, or eat the kind of food that I serve at most catered events. But since I appear as guest chef at the Community Center only once or twice a year, my goal is to make this dinner as delicious and enjoyable as all the other dinners I cater.

Picking the right menu and knowing the relative cost of various ingredients is key.

It helps to think of some world cuisines where people rely on less expensive ingredients for their diets. Beans and rice are staples for most of the world, and the menu I recently served featured Tuscan Bean Soup, and a braised chicken leg with couscous and vegetables.

Chicken breast is relatively expensive, but the dark leg meat is less than half the price, and to my mind much tastier. On a cold night, a hearty braised dish that combines protein, vegetables and starch in one bowl is particularly appealing. It is the kind of satisfying, old fashioned, home cooked meal that one all

Chicken Niçoise (Serves 4)

Ingredients

4 chicken legs (thigh with drumstick)

Vegetable oil

1 Spanish onion, finely sliced

3 ribs celery, diced

1 zucchini, cut into fourths. Remove seeds in center, and dice

1 t minced garlic

1 yellow squash cut into fourths. Remove seeds in center, and dice

1 bunch fresh thyme, finely chopped

2 cups peeled diced tomatoes

2 t pitted black olives

1 t capers

1 cup white wine

Directions

1. In a heavy bottomed pan, brown the chicken legs in a little vegetable oil for about 4 minutes on each side, until well browned.

2. Remove the chicken from the pan and lower the flame. Brown onions on moderate heat, then add the celery, zucchini, and yellow squash, and brown for 3 minutes.

3. Add the garlic, thyme, tomatoes, olives, capers and wine. Then add the chicken back into the pan.

4. Cover and let simmer for about 45 minutes on moderate heat, until chicken starts to fall off the bone.

5. Serve chicken with vegetables in a bowl over couscous.

too rarely encounters in a restaurant, let alone a community dinner. Our task is not merely to fill the belly, but to warm the soul.

Confessions and Conversions

W<small>E ALL HAVE SOME FOODS</small> that we are embarrassed to enjoy, and others that we find unappealing, no matter how many times we have tried them. A variety of factors may be at work, including family preferences and cultural biases, as well as social pressure and current food fads.

Just recently I became an arugula convert, after many years of avoiding these greens. In my case it wasn't that I didn't like the flavor; I had a more practical objection. As a chef I found it endlessly frustrating that arugula would wilt and turn lifeless after just a day or two in the refrigerator, which made it difficult to use on a restaurant menu. In one of the clearest examples of how using locally raised produce makes a difference, the baby arugula grown by *Equinox Farm* in Sheffield remains vital and lively for days. Because of its freshness, it now makes an appearance on the Castle Street menu, in a mix with shaved fennel and oranges underneath a slab of grilled salmon.

Exactly the opposite is true of iceberg lettuce, as it lasts forever in the refrigerator. Upscale restaurants and chefs who serve organically raised and locally produced salad greens are not supposed to admit to liking the stuff, but I do. Perhaps even worse, though we make and serve vinaigrettes made from the finest extra virgin olive oils, cold pressed nut oils and aged vinegars, my dressing

of choice on a slab of iceberg is Russian dressing.

One might imagine that chefs who are surrounded by a vast array of food indulge themselves on whatever they choose, whenever they want to. We are notorious noshers, tasting bits of food as we work, and we also have the responsibility of producing a staff meal every day, which we may partake of as well. But a restaurant kitchen can also be a tense, busy place, with telephones ringing, deliveries arriving, dishes in the midst of preparation, and cooks requiring supervision, all of which make for a less than relaxing and satisfying atmosphere to eat. The interruptions are constant, which means that by the end of the night I have not really eaten dinner. When I go home where it is quiet and peaceful, I often just have a bowl of cereal.

I don't think I scarcely even saw an avocado until I went away to college, at which point it was love at first taste. For some unknown reason, my terrific cook of a mother never bought them, and they were never part of our cuisine. As delicious as they are, avocadoes can also be enormously frustrating, particularly on restaurant menus. They are so frequently too hard, or at the other extreme of black and soft, only having a few days of optimal eating conditions. The frozen avocado that is used in most inexpensive and fast food restaurants is a poor substitute for the real thing.

The increasing availability of locally raised meats on small farms has fostered the emergence of restaurants that pride themselves on being "nose to tail," meaning they buy whole animals from local farmers and butcher the meat themselves. The old butcher's joke is that the only part of the pig that isn't eaten is the squeal, yet many of the rest of us may not be interested in eating offal and organ meat. It has become fashionable for trendy restaurants to feature menu items like trotters and salads with crispy fried pigs' ears, but the clientele for these dishes is limited at best.

Chefs must balance a responsibility to cook a diverse mix of foods that appeal to the general dining public, while also honoring their own sense of taste. Not every dish that appears on the menu may be something I personally enjoy eating. One of the signature ingredients that have come to define new American cooking over the past few decades is locally produced goat cheese. From the earliest days of California cuisine to the present, goat cheese has been ubiquitous in contemporary cooking. In the Berkshires the goat cheese produced by *Rawson Brook Farm* is beloved and has a devoted following. It indeed appears prominently on the Castle Street menu, yet the taste for goat cheese is not one I have managed to acquire, no matter how many times I have tried. The same is true for blue cheese. It's all I can do to touch the stuff, let alone eat it. But I wouldn't deprive my diners of the opportunity to eat it, and I recognize that many others enjoy it. It's all in a chef's work.

Curtains Up

W E WAIT MOST OF THE YEAR in the Berkshires for the summer season to begin, and then suddenly the curtain rises and the season is upon us. Compared to 25 years ago when the Café first opened, the arts season is much longer, extending from spring through fall, and not just in July and August. Barrington Stage Company, Berkshire Theatre Festival, and Shakespeare and Company have all significantly expanded, with months of additional programming, and both the Colonial Theatre and The Mahaiwe present shows year round. That's quite a change from when *Koussevitzky* or even Seiji led the BSO.

But there is nothing like the two months a year when Tanglewood and Jacob's Pillow are in session. It is what restaurants, tent rental companies, photographers, DJs, waiters and bartenders, landscapers and photographers all live for. We plan, anticipate, and gear up for this, and almost as suddenly as it arrives, the season is over. This is certainly truer in Lenox—where many stores and restaurants close for an extended period during the winter—than in Great Barrington, which manages to maintain a greater level of activity year round.

The season brings with it openings, galas, and parties, many of which are catered by area businesses. Virtually every arts, cultural, and nonprofit organization has a fundraising event at some point, and these events attract many of the same people who patronize and support local establishments. For restaurants and caterers, galas and parties are very high profile events; a chance to shine, and an opportunity to show off. The stakes and expectations are high, and the pressure to perform is enormous. It's far easier to come up short by running out of food or failing to provide good service than it is to meet expectations. Bad weather can make even the best food and service seem substandard. Of course, food always tastes better on a beautiful sunny day.

It's often a mad rush to feed guests who are either about to attend a scheduled performance, or who are getting out from a show and are famished and dying for

a drink. The key to handling these events is a huge staff. It is not possible to set up, serve, and feed a large crowd without a small army. In order to avoid long lines at the bar and delays in serving dinner, a caterer must plan for sufficient staff to handle the demands of the event. The single greatest reason why large catered events are less than successful is because of inadequate staff, and that is a lesson I learned long ago.

Eye-catching presentation is also a must, particularly for buffets. Food is transformed when displayed in large quantities. A small bundle of asparagus isn't very impressive sitting on a plate, but a bushel artfully arranged on a huge platter is, even more so if it is sitting on a gorgeous slab of glistening marble. I recently bought a large piece of unfinished 3" thick solid maple, which makes an impressive carving board and helps make any food served on it look appealing.

Of course the food must be bountiful, seasonal, delicious, and interesting. They don't call them "rubber chicken dinners" for nothing. When appropriate, and the summer months of the Berkshire season are precisely those times, serving food at room temperature makes sense. You don't have to worry about cooking on site, and grilled or marinated vegetables, salads, poached or smoked salmon or carved beef tenderloin all work well. As an increasing number of people refrain from eating meat, having a great selection of salads and vegetables has never been more important. I always make a point of serving some less commonly eaten vegetables, like celery root, golden beets, shaved or grilled fennel, Belgian endive, French lentils, or baby bok choy, just to liven things up.

One of the most popular entrees at gala dinners remains beef tenderloin, or filet mignon. It signifies elegance, is always tender, cooks easily, and yields uniform

Roasted Filet Mignon (Serves 8-10)

Ingredients

1 whole beef tenderloin
2 t minced garlic
1 cup vegetable oil
⅓ cup balsamic vinegar
2 t minced fresh rosemary
Salt and pepper

Directions

1. Have your butcher trim a whole beef tenderloin, removing the thin layer of silver membrane on the top. Remove any excess fat, and trim about 1-2'" off the thin end, and reserve for other uses.

2. Combine the oil, vinegar, garlic and rosemary in a bowl, and marinate the meat in this mix for a minimum of 6 hours, or up to several days. Turn occasionally so the mix coats all sides of the meat.

3. Remove the meat from the marinade, drain well, and brown on all sides on a grill, or in a sauté pan, for about 2 minutes on each side.

4. Place the beef on roasting pan, and roast in a 350° oven for about 15-20 minutes for rare, or an internal temperature of 125° on a meat thermometer.

5. Remove the beef from the oven, wrap in aluminum foil, and let sit for 15 minutes. Slice into medallions, and serve immediately. The meat can be served hot or warm.

slices, for either plated or buffet dinners. A whole beef tenderloin is about the size of your arm, and serves 8-12, depending on what else is on the menu. It is delicious either hot or warm, and almost certainly on some gala menu this year.

Evolution of a Dish, or 6 Degrees of Kevin Bacon

PEOPLE ASK ME all the time where I get ideas for new menu items. The sources of inspiration are many. I may eat out at another restaurant and get an idea, see something in one of the many cooking magazines I read, or notice a restaurant review that mentions a dish that sounds interesting. But perhaps the most frequent source for new ideas about food comes from the many local farmers and food purveyors who flourish in the Berkshires, and who take great pride in their products. The following is the story of the evolution of one such dish.

At a recent gathering of *Berkshire Grown* chefs and farmers, I was introduced to Amy from *Cricket Creek Farm* in Williamstown. They make several varieties of

cheese, and raise grass fed beef, and Amy had brought a sample of her aged cow's milk cheese, which she calls *"Maggie's Round."* It's a delicious, firm and buttery cheese, which could have many different uses. Although the Berkshires have local goat cheese from *Rawson Brook Farm*, and Berkshire *Blue Cheese*, for some time I had wondered why someone didn't make a more mainstream cow's milk cheese, like a Swiss or cheddar. "Maggie's Round" fits the bill perfectly.

During the winter we offered a breast of chicken stuffed with Berkshire Blue, wrapped with prosciutto, and served with a roasted fig sauce. While delicious, it was too rich for the spring and summer. I like to serve some type of stuffed chicken breast on the menu because chicken is so popular, and it's the kind of slightly more complicated dish that many home cooks may not bother to make. When I became aware of the *Cricket Creek Farm* cheese, it was exactly the kind of local ingredient I was searching for, and wanted to feature on my menu.

We began stuffing a thinly pounded breast of chicken with some caramelized onions, shredded Maggie's Round cheese, and roasted tomatoes. For a week or two we topped the chicken with sautéed ramps, which are like wild scallions, from *Bar None Ranch* across the border in New York State. But ramps are only available for a few short weeks of spring, and we soon needed a sauce to finish the dish. I wanted to make a fresh tomato and basil salsa to spoon lightly on top, but it was still too early to get a real tomato. There are many ways to sauce any given dish. A sauce made from sherry wine vinegar, fresh thyme, and veal stock works well. The vinegar helps balance the richness of the cheese. But in the summer we will likely change the dish once local tomatoes are available.

The original idea was to make the dish without any meat other than the chicken. One of the reasons many people choose to eat chicken is because they don't want to eat beef or pork, and I didn't want to alienate those diners. Then Kevin Bacon entered the picture. Kevin was the featured star of this year's *Berkshire International Film Festival*, and Castle Street Café was host-ing a dinner in his honor. We just had to sneak a little bacon into the menu somewhere. We decided to wrap the chicken in a strip of bacon, which not only imparts that great smoky, "bacony" flavor, but it also adds some crispness to the outer layer. Perhaps even more impor-tantly, it helps keep the chicken wrapped up tightly and prevents it from unrolling. So it's not just a silly sop to Hollywood, but actually improves the dish, although it could be omitted if anyone didn't want to eat the bacon.

I wouldn't presume to say yet that the dish is in its final form. Like many other dishes, they evolve over time.

Stuffed Chicken Breast Wrapped in Bacon (Serves 4)

Ingredients

4 boneless skinless chicken breasts cut in half

½ cup roasted tomatoes

1 cup shredded Maggie's Round cheese (or Gouda or other cheese)

1 Spanish onion, well sautéed

8 strips of raw bacon

1 t finely chopped fresh thyme

Olive oil

Salt and pepper

¼ cup sherry wine vinegar

1 cup veal or chicken stock

Directions

1. Preheat oven to 350°

2. Cut the chicken breasts in half down the middle, and remove any fat. Cover the meat with some plastic wrap, and pound with a meat mallet, taking care not to tear the meat.

3. Lay the 8 half pieces of chicken breast on the counter, and divide the roasted tomato, cheese, and onions evenly among the chicken pieces.

4. Roll the chicken up as tightly as possible. Use a toothpick if need be to keep it together while wrapping it in bacon.

5. Wrap the bacon around the chicken, trying to keep the seam of the chicken rolled up as much as possible.

6. In a large skillet, heat a tablespoon of olive oil, and place the chicken in the skillet. Season the chicken with salt, pepper, and fresh thyme, and brown on all sides.

7. Place the entire skillet in the oven for about 8 minutes, or until done.

8. Remove the skillet from the oven, place on top of the stove, and add the sherry wine vinegar and stock to the pan. Allow the liquid to reduce by half, and then serve immediately with the sauce.

Recipes and Technique

AS A PROFESSIONAL CHEF and someone who writes recipes on a regular basis, I am frequently asked for recipes for specific dishes. There are no secrets in the kitchen and I am happy to provide these. It is gratifying to know I inspired someone else to cook. At the same time, it is important to recognize the limitations of recipes, and the importance of technique.

Our intrigue often begins because we taste something we'd like to recreate or when looking through a magazine and some recipe or photo strikes our attention. Perhaps you have seen or tasted something while dining out that you'd like to figure out how to make. When preparing a recipe for the first time, it's always a sound idea to initially follow the directions exactly, just to see what the result will be. You need a base from which to begin before you start taking liberties and follow your

own inspiration. This is particularly true in the realm of baking, where modifying recipes is far more likely to yield unsuccessful results than with soups, sauces, and other forms of cooking.

Nonetheless, I also caution against following recipes slavishly and ignoring your own judgment and sense of taste. You are ultimately cooking for yourself and your sense of taste, and it is important to know your own palate and to follow its desires. Some modifications are simple and less risky. Not a fan of spicy food? It's easy to eliminate the hot chilies and crushed red pepper from some international dishes, yet still retain the essential flavor. Curry does not necessarily have to cause sweat to break out on your forehead. Do you have children who don't eat nuts or raisins? Most baked goods that call for these can still be made without them, even if the results are not as tasty. Desserts that taste too sweet can usually be made with less sugar.

Many times a recipe contains a kernel of an idea, or a combination of flavors or seasonings that can be applied to other ingredients to make a dish more to your liking. For example, the essence of many Mediterranean seafood recipes is the classic combination of garlic, tomato, saffron and fennel with shellfish. But if you are allergic to shellfish or just plain squeamish about eating things with tentacles, the same flavor combinations can be combined quite successfully with salmon or flatfish. The essence of Thai and Vietnamese cuisine

Steamed Trout (or other fish) in a Chinese Bamboo Steamer (Serves 1)

Ingredients

6 large kale leaves	½ red pepper, sliced
1 boneless, headless brook trout	½ yellow squash, sliced
½ cup broccoli florets	1 portabella mushroom cap, sliced
	1 t minced ginger

Directions

1. Line the bottom of the steamer basket with kale leaves.

2. Place the trout, skin side down, in the center of the bamboo steamer.

3. Arrange the sliced vegetables around the fish.

4. Fill a skillet with 1" of water, then add the ginger to the water. Place the bamboo basket on the skillet, and then a cover on top of the basket

5. Steam the basket for 5-7 minutes, and check the fish for doneness.

Serve hot, with the Asian Dipping Sauce

Asian Dipping Sauce

Ingredients

1 T brown sugar	½ cup water
½ cup light soy sauce	1 t minced garlic
	1 t minced ginger

Directions

1. Combine the soy sauce and sugar in a small sauce pan and bring to a boil, mixing well, to dissolve the sugar.

2. Add the remaining ingredients and mix well.

is the vibrant combination of mint, basil, ginger, garlic and cilantro. You can use these flavors with just about any main ingredient, depending on whether you are a vegetarian, meat, or fish eater. Keeping records of your recipe changes is critical if you want to remember how you made something a year or two from now.

Those watching their intake of fat and cholesterol are always looking for ways to modify recipes to suit their particular diet. Yes, fat, sugar and butter may be reduced or eliminated from various dishes, but don't expect a Fettuccini Alfredo made with low fat milk and half the cheese to taste the same as one made with heavy cream and plenty of cheese.

Before you try out anything on unsuspecting dinner guests, it's always wise to taste it yourself. One of the most common mistakes of even professional chefs is the tendency to combine too many things together in the same dish. How many times have you dined out and either eaten or seen listed on the menu something like grilled halibut with poached figs and a vanilla, thyme and Sauterne sauce, served over garlic mashed potatoes? The same dish with one or two fewer ingredients would no doubt be better. The virtue of simplicity is sometimes one of the hardest to learn.

Some of the worst excesses of nouvelle cuisine involve inexperienced chefs using trendy ingredients and untried flavor combinations in an effort to attract attention and gain notoriety for creativity. But there's a reason why black pepper ice cream and smoked salmon served with diced kiwis and pink peppercorns are no longer part of the general repertoire. That's why some dishes are classics, and why we keep going back to them.

Using a Chinese bamboo steamer to cook fish is simple, but not widely used in this country. That is a shame, because the baskets are inexpensive and versatile, and a healthy way to cook.

These steamers come in a variety of sizes, and are widely available in Asian specialty stores. For steamed fish, you need a 9-12" steamer.

Steaming is a very forgiving method of cooking. Unlike baking, grilling, or broiling, which dry food out, steaming adds moisture. You can steam almost any selection of vegetables with the fish — broccoli, red peppers, mushrooms, squash, and string beans all work well. If you are uncertain whether or not the fish is cooked, just insert a knife into the flesh and inspect. Thicker pieces of fish will obviously take more time. An Asian style soy dipping sauce is the perfect accompaniment.

A Culinary Challenge

B Y NOW, those of us in the restaurant business are very accustomed to getting special requests from diners on restricted diets. We already indicate which items on the menu are vegetarian, vegan, and gluten free. But that is just the tip of the iceberg, which is why the local Board of Health requires chefs to be certified in Allergy Awareness. For those with severe and life-threatening allergies, to nuts or shellfish for example, extreme care must be used to avoid contaminating food. Sometimes a diner gives me such an extensive list of food that must be avoided — including eggs, dairy, soy, nuts, and wheat — that I am reluctant to serve them. It can be very hard to guarantee their safety in a busy restaurant.

Recently I received a request from someone who dines in the Café quite often. She does so in part because she is on a gluten free diet, and we easily accommodate that request. But in addition to not eating gluten, she also does not eat dairy or chocolate, and she wanted to know if we could make her a gluten free, dairy free dessert without chocolate.

I confess that at first I was dumbfounded, since those restrictions rule out so many desserts. Our fabulous flourless chocolate mousse cake is gluten free, but she can't eat chocolate. We have several other gluten free desserts, like crème brûlée and a frozen lemon soufflé, but they contain diary. Virtually all of the standard dessert repertoire would have to be eliminated, including cakes, pies, tarts, mousses, and custards. What was left?

What's left is fruit, but neither of us wanted to settle for something as pedestrian as a bowl of berries. You don't have to go out to a restaurant to get that. The question was how to augment and embellish some berries so they became more worthy of serving in a restaurant.

There are several approaches. When pineapples are peeled, sliced in discs, and cored, the hole in the center functions the same way as a golf tee does-holding a scoop of sorbet, the whole dish can be garnished with mint, fresh berries, and a fruit sauce to make an elegant dessert.

Another solution involves both sorbet and *dacquoise* (the French word for a meringue, or beaten egg whites, with ground nuts folded in). The nuts give the meringue a pleasant chewiness, less brittle than plain meringue. Dacquoise is simple to make, and since many recipes call for only egg yolks, it is not difficult to accumulate the egg whites you will need. You can use a pastry bag to pipe out 2-3" discs of the dacquoise on a baking pan.

In classical French cuisine, dacquoise is combined with butter cream and chocolate to make a rich, show-stopper dessert that is one of my personal favorites. Sadly, from my perspective, my customer could not eat this. However, fruit sorbet contains no dairy, and it makes a perfect filling for a sandwich in between two layers of dacquoise cookies. Served with a fruit puree, and topped with fresh berries, it is a colorful and elegant dessert that would satisfy any diner.

Hazelnut Dacquoise

Ingredients

⅓ cup sugar	1 tbsp. corn starch
¾ cup hazelnuts, toasted and finely ground	6 egg whites
	pinch salt

Directions

1. Preheat oven to 325°

2. Line a baking pan with parchment paper and trace eight 3" circles on the paper.

3. Place the egg whites into the bowl of an electric mixer, and gently heat over a very low flame or hot water bath until warm to the touch.

4. Add a pinch of salt to the whites, start whipping them, and slowly add the sugar. Beat until firm.

5. Fold in the corn starch and ground nuts.

6. Transfer the mixture to a pastry bag and fill in the 3" circles on the parchment paper, a half-inch deep.

7. Bake 20-25 minutes, until dry.

8. Let cool, and then fill with sorbet and/or fresh fruit.

Asparagus Aspic

VERY FEW PEOPLE eat aspic anymore, or even know what it is. Aspic is simply gelatin, which can be used to coat and decorate food, or which is used to set vegetables in a mold. Some large hotels and cruise ships still feature extravagant buffets, with whole salmon in aspic, garnished with flowers made out of vegetables, but for the most part it is an old fashioned vehicle for preparing and serving food. In fact, aspic is one of the best examples of the kind of overly complicated dish that nouvelle cuisine successfully rebelled against.

However, when I was approached by Chesterwood, the National Historic Landmark home of sculptor Daniel Chester French, to serve a gala dinner there, I was asked to serve a historically accurate dinner that reflected the 1920's entertaining style of Mrs. French.

Chefs and caterers are frequently called upon to provide menus with a theme for special occasions. Wine tasting dinners are one of the most common, requiring chefs to pair food with specific wines, and we are even more frequently called upon to feature locally raised foods for benefit events. Partly because of our location next to the Mahaiwe Theater, we have on several occasions planned menus that are connected to a film. *Babette's Feast* is the most famous, with its turtle soup, and quail in puff pastry –but there are many others. When I was asked to devise a menu before the screening of a summer baseball movie in conjunction with the Berkshire International Film Fes-

tival, a gourmet burger bar, with all the fixings, seemed like the right approach. Sometimes it's easy to find the right menu, other times more difficult. The Chesterwood dinner required a trip down memory lane, for food not commonly served today

As I perused Mrs. French's menu archives, several items stood out — mostly because they are so seldom served today. I haven't seen a croquette listed on a menu in quite some time, which is a shame, really, because they can be delicious when well made. A potato croquette is really just a fried hash brown or mashed potato, which has been fortified with egg, bread crumbs, and parmesan cheese. It makes a great accompaniment to a beef dish, like tournedos of beef, or sliced filet mignon.

The menu item which really caught my eye was aspic. I hadn't made a dish with aspic since cooking school many years ago. Now, asparagus makes a perfect and light first course for dinner, and my natural inclination would be to serve it simply, with vinaigrette, or perhaps with an Asian sesame sauce. But that is not how Mrs. French would have served it. Perhaps an asparagus aspic would have been more to her taste. As I researched recipes, and the dish went through a number of iterations, the final result was a refreshing and unusual dish that makes a first course that stands out and gets your attention – a conversation piece, which is just what is called for on a gala occasion. Like wide neckties, in enough time, aspic might come back in fashion.

Asparagus Aspic (Serves 4)

Ingredients

1½ cups diced raw asparagus spears

2 cups water

1 T sugar

1 T rice wine vinegar

½ t salt

1 envelope unflavored gelatin, dissolved in ½ cup cold water.

¼ cup finely diced carrot

¼ cup finely diced fresh tomato

2 T grated onion

1 T chopped fresh dill

1 cup finely shredded romaine hearts

½ cup finely shredded spinach

¼ cup vegetable oil

1 T rice wine vinegar

¼ cup peeled and diced red tomato

¼ cup peeled and diced yellow tomato

Directions

1. Blanch the asparagus in boiling water for 2 minutes, remove them from the water, and plunge in ice water. Reserve the cooking liquid. *Set aside 4 tablespoons of diced asparagus for garnish.*

2. Combine one cup of the asparagus cooking water with the sugar and rice wine vinegar in a sauce pot, and bring to a boil. Add the softened gelatin, stir well, and place the pot in an ice bath to chill.

3. When the liquid starts to thicken, add the diced asparagus, minced carrot, chopped tomato, grated onion, dill and salt.

4. Pour the mixture into small oiled ramekins, and chill.

5. To serve, combine the shredded romaine heart and spinach with the oil and vinegar, and spread onto four plates. Unmold the ramekins, and center on the plates. Garnish with diced tomato and the reserved asparagus tops.

Mitzvah Meal

AN ELDERLY AUNT OF MINE recently died, leaving behind her spouse of almost 70 years. Like many men of his generation, my uncle didn't do much cooking, at least not until my aunt's condition worsened to the point that she could no longer do it herself. She was an unusually devoted home cook, for whom preparing a thoughtful meal was very important. That is not to say she was a gourmet cook. Later in life she got a degree in nutrition, and her interest was in preparing healthy and nutritious meals. No meal was complete without several different kinds of vegetables. My aunt was strictly old school, preparing renditions of many Eastern European classics, and the tenets of nouvelle cuisine never crept into her kitchen. She took enormous pride and pleasure in watching her son and nephews consume mind-boggling quantities of food. She was never one for dining out in restaurants much either. She believed that her home-cooked meals were better than anything she was likely to encounter in a restaurant.

If you were hoping for a rich dessert at the end of the meal, however, you were in the wrong place. If there is a single phrase of hers I will always remember, it was her admonition against

eating chocolate and fattening foods: *"You don't need it."*

It is a widespread custom almost everywhere to provide food for the grieving after a death in the family, but that usually comes to a halt pretty quickly and people are left on their own. Since my uncle is unsteady on his feet and has trouble walking, a home health care aide was quickly brought in to prepare meals. She is a pleasant woman and adequate cook, but nothing like my aunt. In addition to the loss of friends and family, and the inexorable deterioration of the body, the elderly also often suffer the loss of the kind of home cooked meals they grew up with. This is particularly true for anyone receiving institutional care. My father spent the last months of his life in a nursing home, but was fortunate that my mother lived nearby and was still able to bring him some of his favorite foods. But nonetheless, he often ate the food prepared in the nursing home. I will never forget visiting him once when the evening meal was served, and dinner was canned franks and beans, something he would have never chosen to eat. There weren't very many pleasures left in life for him at that point, and that meal struck me as a particular indignity.

It was with that in mind that I decided to help celebrate my uncle's birthday by bringing an old-fashioned home cooked meal to his house. I wanted something that could be prepared in advance, would travel well, and be the kind of authentic and old-fashioned meal he enjoyed but doesn't get to eat much anymore. Braised short ribs worked perfectly. They require several hours of cooking, but that can be done beforehand, and they reheat easily and quickly. The meat is very soft and tender, and easy to eat. It's the kind of heartwarming meal we don't get nearly enough of anymore, and which we would all do well to share with others.

Braised Short Ribs (Serves 6)

Ingredients

Six 8-10 oz. pieces boneless chuck short rib

thyme, fresh or dry

1 onion, pureed in a food processor

3 carrots, cut into chunks

8 whole shallots or small white pearl onions, peeled

6 crimini (or other) mushrooms, cut into fourths

½ t minced garlic

2 cups tomato paste

1 bottle ketchup

½ cup smoky BBQ sauce

2 cups veal stock (optional)

2-3 cups water

The trick is buying boneless chuck short rib, which I think is even better than bone-in. They have a numerical code that some real butchers might know; it is # 1116G. They are not nearly as fatty as bone in short rib.

Directions

1. Preheat oven to 375°

2. Brown the meat in a braising pot with salt and pepper, and some fresh or dry thyme.

3. Remove the meat and put to the side. Brown the pureed onions, then add garlic, carrots, and mushrooms, and brown for a few more minutes. Add the tomato paste, ketchup, BBQ sauce, (optional veal stock) and then add enough water so it isn't too thick.

4. Add the meat, cover the pot, and bake for about 3 hours in preheated oven until the meat is very tender.

5. You may have to add some more water to the pot if it has reduced too much.

6. Skim off any fat, and serve with mashed potatoes.

Feeding the Birds

As a professional chef, I have spent most of the past 30-odd years engaged in the work of feeding people, which has been a gratifying, enjoyable and rewarding career. I have received my fair share of acclaim and recognition for this, and it has helped shape my identity as well. Among the most satisfying elements is having a great working relationship with staff and employees, and getting to know my regulars, who have been devoted and loyal customers. I am in the business of welcoming the familiar as well as strangers in for a meal, and providing a warm and comfortable place to gather.

Since moving my home to what feels like a glass tree house, perched on a hillside surrounded by forest, I have developed a new clientele. "Clientele" isn't exactly the right word, because unlike the diners in the Café who pay for their food, it is I who bear the cost of feeding the birds. This is something I readily do. It has become an important part of my daily life, and an integral part of my work of providing meals for others. The cold and snowy winter seems a particularly important time to carry on with this work, and my efforts do not go unrecognized. I know the diners in the restaurant appreciate good food, but it is no doubt decorum and the fact that they are not quite so hungry that prevent them from eagerly attacking their meal the way the birds do.

The daily ritual begins with a trip outside with a cupful of feed while the coffee drips. Especially on unusually cold or snowy days, by the time I have walked the few feet from my door to the hanging feeder, I can hear the excited flapping of wings and stirring in the branches. There are times I approach the feeder and can sometimes be literally swarmed by a small flock of birds anticipating breakfast. I enjoy mine and they enjoy theirs. It only seems fair. While some people know and care about the names and variety of species in their feeders, that is not important to me. Yes, I do recognize the chickadees, and even I, who know little about birds, can't miss the blue jays. The blue jay dwarfs in size most of the other birds at the feeder, and easily muscles out anyone in his way. The several pair of mourning doves are also easily identifiable, but the many other varieties whose names I do not know are just as welcome.

Like every other feeder of birds, the squirrels are the bane of my existence. I'm not sure why it seems like an act of charity and mercy to feed the birds and not the squirrels, but it does. They are such unrelenting pigs, and seem so unwilling to share. The birds just seem so much more vulnerable, and their survival in this weather seems miraculous.

Earlier in the winter before the heavy snow fell, the feeder attracted the attention of a large brown bear, who tore down the feeder and walked around my deck like a dog with a Frisbee in its mouth. Now the feeder hangs higher, and the bears are presumably sleeping.

When the warmer weather arrives, the birds will have other dining options, and my role will become less important. But in the meantime, the first meal I serve every day is for the birds.

Honoring Food Traditions

OUR MOST IMPORTANT TRADITIONS call for special or ceremonial foods to help celebrate the occasion. Thanksgiving is almost unthinkable without turkey, Passover calls for chicken soup with matzo balls and macaroons, and lamb or ham are central to many Easter Sunday meals. The holiday simply wouldn't feel right without these traditional foods. We associate some foods so particularly with special occasions that even though they are delicious, we don't often eat them during the rest of the year. Yorkshire pudding is a Christmas favorite with roast beef, and though it's not hard to make, it feels like a dish we reserve for major occasions.

I don't cater many holiday dinners, but I do cater a lot of weddings, and those are the kinds of meals where people feel strongly about honoring their culinary heritage. For many assimilated Americans, that doesn't mean much in particular — chicken, fish, or steak with mashed potatoes and vegetables and a nice salad is all that is required. But I also cater an increasing number of cross-cultural weddings, where it is very important to the family members that their heritage be reflected in the meal. There is a desire to be true to their culture, and serve food that family will recognize and understand. Couples also want to use the occasion to introduce their in-laws and newly acquired family to the culinary culture marrying into the family.

One of the mixed weddings I remember most was a Jewish-Puerto Rican wedding, where the menu consisted of roast pork with black beans, and pot roast with kasha varnishkes (buckwheat groats mixed with bow tie pasta). A few weeks before the wedding, the groom stopped by the Café on a busy Saturday night with a small plastic container of his mother's kasha, just to show me how it should taste. I routinely issue a disclaimer to wedding clients that I will do my best to make what they request, but that my rendition of a dish will almost certainly not be as tasty as their mother's version.

The most recent challenge came from a Vietnamese bride, who explained that she wanted to have an authentic Vietnamese wedding banquet for her wedding reception. Although the groom is American, it was very important to the bride and her family that they serve a

meal that honored their culture. Vietnamese food happens to be one of my favorite Asian cuisines, and I was already somewhat familiar with the seasonings. Vietnamese fish sauce, lime juice, sugar, garlic and chilies are the essential flavors. A traditional Vietnamese wedding meal is in fact a huge, multi-course dinner consisting of 6-10 separate courses, including beef, fish, chicken, noodle, and vegetarian dishes.

I did some research on the internet, and the bride supplied me with some recipes. We arranged for a wedding tasting, and when the bride showed up with her mother, I knew I had a tough audience. Her mother spoke no English, but she managed to convey skepticism about the meal to come. I confess I was more than a little nervous cooking for someone who clearly knew more about her national cuisine than I did. I got a few suggestions about how to make things better or differently, but they approved of the meal, and I was hired to cater the wedding.

The clincher came with dessert. I didn't make the traditional Vietnamese dessert of sweetened bean paste, because I wasn't able to obtain some of the ingredients. I knew they didn't want a western style wedding cake, or rich chocolate dessert. I thought perhaps that they might like a coconut dessert, since that is lighter, and is commonly used in their cooking. With this in mind, when it came time to show the dessert option, I brought out some coconut macaroons for them to try. The mother broke into a broad smile when she tasted the macaroons, and I didn't need to know her language to understand her pleasure. As she left, she pocketed the last remaining cookie and put in her purse. We added the macaroons to the menu — a little traditional Jewish cuisine in an otherwise authentic Vietnamese meal.

The whole time I couldn't help thinking that the

Grilled Quail, Vietnamese Style (Serves 4)

Quail are not commonly eaten in this country today, for two reasons: they are expensive and there isn't much to eat on a quail. It takes 2-3 quail to make a meal, and a lot of picking through tiny bones. Despite the drawbacks, there is still a place for quail at special occasions. They certainly aren't hard to make; if you can make chicken, you can cook quail, just more quickly.

Ingredients

8 quail	2 t chili powder
4 T vegetable oil	2 T sugar
8 scallions, finely chopped	2 t salt
8 cloves of garlic, chopped	2 T Vietnamese fish sauce (Nuoc Mam)
1" piece of lemongrass, chopped	Juice of 2 limes
	4 T water

Directions

1. Heat the vegetable oil in the skillet and fry the garlic, scallions and lemongrass for 2 minutes.

2. Add the chili powder, fish sauce, sugar, salt, water, and lime juice, and simmer for 3 minutes.

3. Let the marinade cool, then marinate the quail for at least 2 hours, or overnight.

4. Heat the grill and cook for 7 minutes on each side, basting frequently with the marinade.

mother was old enough to have lived through the Vietnam War, and that the least I could do was to try my best to prepare a delicious wedding meal for her daughter.

Gathering the Last Fruits of Summer

O N THE FIRST WEEKEND in October one year, the leaves were well on their way to peak color, and it was long past the prime harvest season in the Berkshires. I decided to take advantage of a rare afternoon off to hike to the top of one my favorite spots atop Mount Washington, and enjoy the fall colors.

It's a hike I have taken many times and know well, in part because it's a great place to pick blueberries. Unfortunately, because the height of the summer tourist season in the Berkshires is exactly when blueberries ripen, I don't often get the chance to go wild blueberry picking. It is one of life's regrets that I don't do that more often. So imagine my surprise when, reaching the top of this mountain, I noticed these purple spots in the underbrush. Could there still be ripe blueberries this late in the season? I hadn't seen any berries on the way up, but right at the top, which gets the most sunlight and the most wind exposure, there were still quite a few berries clinging to the bush. Had the birds and the bears been so sated that they left some for me? This was unusually late in the season, and the berries were a little withered. But just as late harvest grapes make for the sweetest wines, blueberries that have ripened this long and have had some of their water evaporate, are more delicious and sweeter than berries picked early in the year.

A chef in a blueberry patch is like Winnie the Pooh at a beehive. The urge to pick wild berries is old and primal. Especially with low bush berries, it really helps to sit on the ground to better see and reach in the brush, just as our ancestors did before they learned to walk upright. It's not just *free* food, it's food of the rarest and highest integrity, and all too difficult to find today. There are no distributors, processors, or delivery guys involved, it's literally hand to mouth. Very few of us eat much food like that anymore.

Most of us stopped being hunter-gatherers a long time ago, but one of the joys of living in the Berkshires is that we can still pick wild berries in season, or go to

Homemade Applesauce

Yields just over a quart

Ingredients

3 lbs. apples (a sweet variety like Macintosh is best)

2½ cups water

¼ cup light brown sugar

¾ t cinnamon

Directions

1. Wash the apples, and slice into quarters.

2. Put the cut apples into a heavy bottomed sauce pot and add the remaining ingredients.

3. Bring to a boil and simmer for 10 minutes.

4. Allow the mix to cool, then puree in a food mill or food processor. If using a food processor, pass the pureed apples through a coarse strainer, to remove the seeds and skin.

pick-your-own orchards to gather fruit. The experience is completely different from buying prepackaged fruit in a crowded, neon lit supermarket. The Berkshires and Hudson Valley have many orchards, and if you didn't pick any of your own berries or fruit this year, you missed out on a rewarding and fun experience. And of course once you've gathered fruit, you can take some home to cook with.

It's easy to get carried away picking apples in a beautiful setting, and many people return from an apple orchard with more apples than they know what to do with. Making applesauce is the perfect use for large quantities of apples. Even without canning, it will last for at least two weeks in the refrigerator and is perfect for serving with roasts, using in baking, and simply eating alone.

Wrestling with Bones

MANY CUSTOMERS and amateur home cooks wonder what it is like to be a professional chef. People frequently ask me how I know how much food to order, or after visiting the Café on a busy night and peeking into the partially open kitchen, wonder how it is possible to serve so many people such different menu items simultaneously. My usual response is: "The same way you get to Carnegie Hall." Aside from the volume of food prepared, perhaps the biggest difference between a Western or European style professional restaurant kitchen and a home kitchen is the making and use of stock.

Most of my days begin and end wrestling with bones. Making stock, particularly dark meat stock, requires a lot of time, space, and strength. One of the first things I do after entering the restaurant is to haul a 50 pound box of beef or veal bones out of the walk in refrigerator, and place them in a large roasting pan about 8 square feet, and roast it in an oven for about 2 ½ hours. This monopolizes an oven for quite a bit of time. In a busy restaurant that does a lot of baking and requires use of the oven for other cooking, this is best done in the morning before dinner service begins.

After the bones are well browned, but not burned, they are removed from the oven, and transferred to large stockpots. Any serious profes-

sional kitchen has at least one large stockpot, which can accommodate about 10 or more gallons of liquid. In addition to the bones, *mirepoix* is added—the French word for the holy trinity of carrots, onion, and celery. Thyme, bay leaves, and peppercorns are also essential ingredients. In addition to the roasting, which darkens the color of the stock, what also makes stock brown is the addition of tomato paste, which thickens the resulting stock.

Making stock is not for the faint of heart, or anyone squeamish about handling a large pile of knees, ankles,

and femurs. While many people think that the valuable part of an animal is the flesh and that the bones are waste, chefs know and value bones for the flavor they impart to food and the stock. It may seem counterintuitive, but bone—and specifically marrow—makes far more flavorful stock than the meat itself. The meat is best roasted, grilled, or sautéed and eaten, with the bones slowly simmered to make stock for soups or sauces.

These large pots of bones require simmering at low temperatures for a long time. Because of the amount of time required and the space they occupy on the stove, they cannot be simmered during the day or while the Café is serving dinner. The large pots are placed in the walk in refrigerator until the end of the evening. Large volumes of liquid are necessary, because by the time the stock is slowly cooked and strained, the final result will yield a much smaller volume of liquid.

After a busy night serving dinner and cleaning up the kitchen afterwards, one of the last tasks to be completed is to retrieve the stockpots from the walk in refrigerator. When loaded with bones, each weigh about 35 pounds and after placing them on the stove, they are filled up with cold water. The stock must be brought to a low simmer, and then the flame turned down very low, so the liquid barely bubbles. The stock simmers slowly overnight, for about 12 hours. It is essential that the flame be adjusted perfectly; too low and the stock doesn't cook, too high and it will boil over during the night risking fire, or burn the bottom of the pot resulting in a burned and acrid flavor.

Upon entering the Café the next morning and opening the door, the first sensation that greets me is the fragrant bouquet of simmering stock, unmistakable anywhere. The next step in making stock is to remove

---

Brown Chicken Stock

Ingredients

4 lbs. chicken bones	2 carrots, diced
1 cup tomato paste	½ head celery chopped
2 gallons cold water	1 bay leaf
1 onion, peeled and sliced	½ t thyme
	Pinch whole black peppercorns

Directions

1. Preheat oven to 350°

2. Roast the bones in a roasting pan for 90 minutes.

3. Remove the bones from the roasting pan, place them in a heavy bottomed sauce pot, and cover with cold water.

4. Pour off any grease from the empty roasting pan, and add some water to the pan. Scrape off any bits from the bottom of the pan, and add to the sauce pot.

5. Add the tomato paste, herbs, and vegetables, and stir well, to mix in the tomato paste.

6. Bring the liquid to a boil, and then simmer gently for 1 hour.

7. Remove the bones, and continue to simmer the liquid until it reduces to about 2 quarts.

8. Strain the stock through a fine sieve, and reserve for later use

---

the bones from the liquid, and discard them. They have imparted their flavor to the liquid, and at this point have no further value, except to large dogs. Well-prepared stock contains virtually no fat. This is because any fat or grease rises to the surface, which is skimmed off and removed. The old expression that scum rises to the top of a boiling pot is literally true in this case. The next step in preparing stock is to bring the liquid to a boil to skim off any impurities, as well as to reduce and concentrate the flavor.

Depending on the intended uses, the stock is further cooked to reduce the volume, which thickens the liquid. The French term is *demi-glace*, literally meaning half stock, or that the volume of liquid is reduced by half. This is what most restaurants make and use, including Castle Street Café. What started out as 10 gallons of thin liquid ends up turning into 5 gallons of rich, highly concentrated flavor. The last and final step in the process is to pass the liquid through a fine, wire mesh strainer, which removes any solids from the stock and ensures a finely textured, smooth liquid. This is the basis for sauces made with wild mushrooms, red wine, roasted garlic, and many other dishes.

From start to finish the process takes somewhere between 24-36 hours. It is a lot of work, and almost no home cooks, no matter how accomplished, make this. It is one of the defining differences between even the most lovingly prepared homemade food, and professionally cooked restaurant food.

There is, however, a way for home cooks to make a similar roasted stock out of chicken bones instead of veal and beef bones. Chicken bones are much less expensive, and the kind of thing you might have around the house if you have roasted a chicken, or buy whole chickens to cook with. Furthermore, the whole process takes less time. Chicken bones don't yield a stock which jells in the same way that stock from beef or veal bones does, but it is much easier to make, and less time consuming. Anyone who has made a simple chicken stock by simmering chicken bones need only roast them first, add some tomato paste to the liquid, and the result will be a stock which is much richer than that made with unroasted bones. Though not as rich as *demi-glace*, it will still make the basis for some delicious home sauces.

Tossed Potatoes

TODAY WE GATHER INFORMATION about new food trends through the internet, but prior to that, simply going out to eat at a new restaurant was the best way to gauge current food trends. As spring arrives, and the season for hiking and camping outdoors is upon us, I was reminded of an old recipe for Tossed Potatoes. It's a dish I have made only once on a camping trip in Olympic National Park along the coast of Washington State.

As anyone who has ever gone camping or backpacking knows, there is nothing that stimulates the appetite more than eating outdoors at the end of a long day. For most of us who live the overwhelming part of our life indoors, it is an exceptional thing to spend a few days almost entirely outdoors. Waking up in a tent, eating meals outside, answering the call of nature in the woods, and returning to sleep again at night outside is all part of the experience. For one thing, the exertion involved in hauling a full backpack loaded with hiking and camping gear is enormous, and the calories expended are far more than in our normal, day-to-day life. Especially in cooler weather, just maintaining body temperature requires a significantly greater consumption of food. When you add in the difficulty of carrying the weight of enough food, combined with the obvious limitations of carrying only dried or non-perishable food, it becomes clear that eating well is a challenge on a camping trip.

Of course there is a variety of high tech, freeze dried foods available at specialty camping stores, but these are expensive, and resemble food designed for the space program rather than a backpacking trip. If the whole point of a camping trip is to immerse oneself in the glories of nature, it is not appealing to eat some freeze dried, reconstituted synthetic food over the campfire. That explains the appeal of timeless classics like peanut butter and jelly, oatmeal, and yes, GORP — good old raisins and peanuts, otherwise known as trail mix. A certain amount of deprivation is part and parcel of any camping trip. It would never occur to me to make instant coffee at home instead of my regular brewed dark roast, but that is an acceptable and sensible alternative on a camping trip. I have seen those who have schlepped their tiny Italian espresso maker into the backwoods, but that seems like an insertion of luxury into what should otherwise be a Spartan experience.

So after a drive from Seattle to the outskirts of Olympic National Park, I stopped in a large grocery store with

my old camping buddy to load up on provisions for our outing in the park. You can buy most of what you need for such a camping trip at the average supermarket. We bought some of the aforementioned provisions, along with some basmati rice, canned tuna, and instant soup mix. Of course we loaded up on chocolate, even more indispensable on a camping trip than in everyday life. It is almost impossible to have too much chocolate on a camping trip, essential for injecting energy into tired bodies that are flagging by late afternoon. We have learned that firm avocados will survive the first couple of days of jostling on a camping trip pretty well, and they introduce fresh produce into an otherwise dried diet. It must have been in the produce department that I spied the red bliss potatoes and thought they would make a delicious addition to the menu. They could easily be shoved into some small pack pocket.

From the grocery store we headed into the park. Olympic National Park includes a spectacular 100-mile section of coastline, along which hikers alternate walking on the beach with hiking over the cliffs, depending on the tides. It is one of the most remote places on the continent I have ever been, with huge pieces of driftwood washing up on the beach. Just off the shore lay the distinctive rock totems, which is all that remains of earlier coastal erosion. Bald eagles can be seen circling overhead, and offshore sea lions and seals bask on the rocks.

While it is spectacularly beautiful and remote, it takes a lot of effort to get there — three days of solid hiking from the nearest access point. I have learned from experience that even the shortest and easiest exertion will serve to leave the rest of the teeming masses behind, and we had succeeded in our effort to find silence and solitude.

In our earlier shopping zeal, we had significantly overestimated the quantity of food even we would consume in a few days, and by the last night it was obvious we would not be eating the red potatoes. As appealing as they seemed boiled, with limited stove fuel, we had not gotten around to eating them. Our feet were blistered, and we knew exactly how arduous the hike back would be. The idea of carrying out anything not absolutely necessary on our sore backs filled us with dread. In a flash of inspiration, standing on the edge of America on the Pacific Coast, we devised our recipe for Tossed Potatoes. Getting as close to the water without getting our feet wet, we hurled them as far as we could into the surf.

PART II

Favorite Recipes

· ·

Gazpacho for the Soul

AFTER 30 YEARS in the restaurant business, it still shocks me how few people enjoy cold soup. In the heat and humidity of high summer, few things are more appealing to me. Conversely, while a hot bowl of homemade soup is very comforting when it's cold out, it is not what I desire when it's warm. As much as I enjoy eating classics like coq au vin and cassoulet in the winter, in the summer a simple salad and bowl of cold soup is what I want to eat. We New Englanders simply don't need to eat as much when it is 90 degrees outside, compared to the dead of winter. Although few of us really modify our diets accordingly, an enormous percentage of our daily caloric intake goes to maintaining body temperature. Eskimos need to consume more calories than South Seas islanders.

I know from prior experience that during ski season and when it is frigid outside, hot soup is a big seller in the Café. Hot soup satisfies a primal craving for warmth. But for some reason, the opposite doesn't seem to be as true in summer. When it is blisteringly hot and oppressively humid, cold soup doesn't resonate in the same way. There is no best seller *Gazpacho for the Soul* like there is *Chicken Soup for the Soul*. Yes, it is true, during peak tomato season gazpacho is popular, and I make it regularly. But it is a very short season, and unless very ripe local tomatoes are available, it is unthinkable to even attempt to make this soup. There is virtually no such thing as tomatoes that are too ripe. When tomato season comes, local farmers often sell bruised, split, or cracked tomatoes at a discount. These are perfect for soup, and less expensive.

It is simple to blanch and peel a tomato: simply remove the core with a paring knife, and then drop in boiling water for 15 seconds, then plunge into ice water. The skin then easily peels off, and you're ready to make soup or sauce.

The season is all too fleeting, so make the most of it while it is here. It will give your soul goose bumps.

Gazpacho (Serves 6)

Ingredients

4 large ripe tomatoes	1 T finely chopped basil
1 cucumber, peeled and seeded	1 T finely chopped parsley
½ small red onion	3 T extra virgin olive oil
½ t minced garlic	2 T balsamic vinegar
6 oz. V-8 or tomato juice	Tabasco or hot sauce to taste
1 bunch scallions, minced	

Directions

1. Remove the core of the tomato. Score the bottom of the tomato with an "X" mark, and drop in boiling water for 15 seconds. Then plunge in ice water.

2. Peel the skin off, cut the tomato in half, and squeeze out the seeds.

3. Place the tomato, cucumber, red onion, and garlic in a blender or food processor, and puree.

4. Add the remaining ingredients, and taste for salt and pepper. Serve well chilled, with some minced scallion or herbs on top.

A Hill of Beans

ONE OF THE MORE COMMON IDIOMS in English to express contempt or derision is to say that something doesn't amount to a hill of beans, as if a hill of beans isn't worth very much. On the contrary, in many parts of the world a hill of beans is the staple of life, and the major source of protein. Many Americans regard meat as a necessary source of protein, when in fact beans can provide a plentiful amount.

I have been pleased and surprised to see that the new Southwestern Black Bean burger we have been serving in the Café has been so popular. Of course we have been serving locally raised grass fed beef burgers from *Ioka Valley Farm* for years, but there are an increasing number of diners who want a vegetarian burger. Only a few years ago we put a vegetarian burger on the menu, but soon removed it because so few people ordered it. What a difference a few years make!

In addition to being vegetarian, this black bean burger is vegan and wheat free, and there has been an enormous increase in diners who are vegan and avoid gluten. The entire dish is Southwestern in style, and rather than serve the burger on a roll, it is served on a

crispy corn tortilla. Served with both a green tomatillo sauce and a more traditional tomato salsa with cilantro, it's topped with guacamole.

The sauces are essential, because they provide both moisture and sharply contrasting flavors, and the combination of the two creates a flavor sensation greater than the sauces separately. Even though sour cream would seem to be a natural component of this dish, I omit it from the serving to keep the whole dish vegan, though one could easily add it.

Over time I think that more people for a variety of different reasons will chose to reduce the quantity of meat they eat, and that increasing numbers of people will be choosing to eat gluten free. Vegetarian burgers are here to stay. Fortunately, this one is tasty, and easy to make.

Southwestern Bean Burger

(Makes 10-12 Burgers)

Ingredients

¾ cup dry mushrooms — save liquid after soaking

6 cups cooked black beans

3 T chopped garlic

2 ¾ cups oats

6 t chili powder

3 t cumin

3 T soy sauce

1 bunch cilantro

Directions

1. Preheat oven to 325°

2. Soak the mushrooms in hot water, drain and save the liquid.

3. Puree mushrooms and remaining ingredients in a food processor, adding mushroom liquid as needed.

4. Form into burger patties.

5. Bake for 10 minutes in preheated oven.

6. Serve on a corn tortilla with sauces and guacamole.

Tomato Salsa

Ingredients

2 cups fresh tomatoes- peeled, diced, and then chopped

1 t minced garli

½ red onion, minced finel

1 bunch scallions, finely chopped

1 bunch cilantro, finely chopped

2 T olive oil

2 T red wine vinegar

Salt and Tabasco sauce to taste

Directions: Mix all the ingredients together.

Tomatillo Salsa Verde

Ingredients

1 lb. tomatillos (small green tomatoes)

1 Spanish onion sliced

1 bunch cilantro

1 T chopped garlic

Splash rice wine vinegar

Salt and Tabasco to taste

Directions

1. Peel off outer papery skin on the tomatillos.

2. In a small saucepot, combine the tomatillos and onion, and simmer for about 10 minutes until soft.

3. Puree with the garlic and cilantro in a food processor, or blender. Add vinegar, salt and Tabasco to taste.

Happy Foods

IF I HAVE LEARNED ANYTHING AT ALL in over 30 years working as a chef, it is that there are a couple of nearly universal "Happy Foods." By that I mean foods that bring an almost childlike joy and smile to almost everyone. They are foods from childhood that we continue to love in almost the same way, even when we are older. The sad reality is that today many people have so much anxiety about food that eating brings no joy at all. Worries about cholesterol, gluten, carbohydrates, allergies, adulterated and unnatural food, and animal welfare are just some of the issues that preoccupy increasing numbers of eaters, and that diminish the joy of eating.

Spinach may be the source of Popeye's power, and healthy to boot, but I doubt it is among the foods that commonly bring happiness to most people. I love great homemade bread fresh from the oven while still hot, and while it is satisfying and comforting, I don't think of it as being joyous. Even more than the British, we are a nation of Beefeaters. Millions of us are sustained on burgers every day, but even among those with no qualms about eating humanely raised animals, eating meat is inherently serious.

Summer is the high season for two of what I think of as being the happiest of foods.

What makes me happy, and a lot of other people happy, is ice cream and watermelon. Two of the most important attributes, if not requirements, of Happy Food are sweetness and juiciness. Happy Food has a lot of moisture. It is instantly satisfying in a way that drier food is not. We sapiens are over 90 percent water, and especially in the heat of summer, we need to drink a lot. After a hot and busy summer night in the Café, I have witnessed many times how a wedge of cold watermelon can bring instant joy and happiness to a tired and sweaty staff. Even the most sober and upright find it hard not to grin with juice running down their chin. Generally cantaloupes are not as sweet as watermelons, but in recent years I have had some intoxicating and almost alcoholically sweet melons from *Farm Girl Farm* that were wonderfully messy and juicy to eat. We're also geneti-

cally predisposed to be attracted to sweetness. Nothing is as primal or satisfying as ice cream on a hot summer day. We have all seen long lines at local ice cream parlors on scorching hot days, and they are not all kids. Even though the drive to maintain warmth is more powerful than the need to cool down most times, I don't think a bowl of hot soup on a cold winter day creates as much happiness for most people as a bowl of ice cream on a hot day.

Of course the glaring exception to the rule that Happy Food has moisture is chocolate. But it is sweet, and oh so satisfying, and right at the top of the list of Happy Foods.

Making homemade ice cream is one of the most happiness inducing experiences there is. It's not hard at all, and fun no matter how old you are. Luddite that I am, I have a fondness for the old-fashioned machine, which requires ice and rock salt, though countertop models work just as well. In the Berkshires, we are blessed with the incredible cream from *High Lawn Farm*, which has a very high butterfat content that is ideal for making ice cream.

'Tis the season. Who needs anti-depressants when you can make homemade ice cream?

Homemade Vanilla Ice Cream (Makes 1 quart)

Ingredients

2 cups milk	6 egg yolks
1 vanilla bean	1 cup heavy cream
1 cup sugar	2 t vanilla extract

Directions

1. Cut the vanilla bean in half lengthwise, and scald in hot milk for a few minutes to soften.

2. Scrape out the seeds from the bean, and return to the milk. Keep warm over low heat.

3. Beat yolks and sugar together, add extract, and then add hot milk. Beat well.

4. Cook yolk and milk mixture over low heat while constantly stirring, until mixture thickens and is warm to the touch. Be careful not to scramble eggs.

5. Place the mix in an ice bath to cool down, and add cold cream.

6. Churn in machine.

To make espresso ice cream: Delete vanilla bean and extract, and after scalding milk, add ½ cup ground espresso to the milk and let it steep for 5 minutes. Strain out coffee through a fine filter, then repeat steps 2-5 above.

Soup

SOUP PLAYS A UNIQUE and distinctive role in many restaurants. It is often the main menu item that the wait staff gets a chance to really eat. A well-run restaurant provides samples of menu specials for waiters to taste so they can explain new dishes to diners, but that is usually only a small taste. In most of the restaurants I have worked in, waiters could have relatively generous samples of soup. One of the ways a chef can inspire confidence in servers is by having the soup be delicious. Since wait staff don't generally have much opportunity to taste a lot of the other menu items, it is that much more important for the soup to be delicious. I have seen numerous servers show up for their shift and start out by tasting the soup du jour.

If you walked into the kitchen of many American households just a generation or two ago in the dead of winter, you would have likely found a kettle of soup simmering on the stove. As a child I recall many a roast chicken dinner in which the carcass and leftover bones became the basis of a flavorful broth. Especially because soup and stockpots tend to be oversized and don't fit easily in the refrigerator, our porch served as an extra refrigerator in winter. The congealed fat was easily separated when chilled, yielding a clear delicious broth. The bouquet of simmering soup can fill a home and provide anticipation of a great meal to come. Soup is frequently better on the second or third day, as the flavors mellow.

When it is bone chilling cold in New England, you need a hearty substantial soup to keep warm, and one based on cabbage is just the ticket. Unlike heirloom tomatoes and precious baby lettuces, cabbage is not one of the chic vegetables. With the hopes of changing that, I

offer the following recipe. It is remarkably inexpensive, almost incomprehensibly so. I recently bought some enormous heads of cabbage the size of a basketball for just a few dollars, which was enough to make soup for a dozen. If you are a fan of stuffed cabbage, you can remove the largest outer leaves and use them to make stuffed cabbage, and use the remainder for soup.

Rustic Cabbage Soup (Serves 6-8)

Ingredients

1 head green cabbage	1 T dill seed
2 Spanish onions, thinly sliced	1 bunch dill, finely chopped
vegetable oil	Salt and pepper
½ cup flour	1 cup heavy cream
1 Qt. chicken stock	2 T soy sauce

Directions

1. Cut the cabbage in half and remove the core. Slice or shred the cabbage into small pieces.

2. In a heavy bottomed saucepot, brown the onions in a little vegetable oil on low heat for about 5 minutes, until golden.

3. Add the cabbage, and stir and cook for another 5 minutes.

4. Add the flour, and stir well, scraping from the sides and bottom.

5. Pour in the chicken stock, stir well and add the dill seed.

6. Let the soup simmer for 20 minutes.

7. Add the chopped dill, heavy cream and the soy sauce. Season with salt and pepper.

8. Serve hot with good bread.

In Praise of Braising

IN THE DEPTHS OF WINTER we are drawn to the hearth and the warmth of the kitchen, and to eating a heartier cuisine. Since an enormous percentage of our caloric intake is devoted to maintaining body temperature, it is only natural that we require more fuel in the winter. This is the time of year for slow food, and there is no better example of that than slowly cooked braised food. Some of the classic dishes of European cuisine are based on braising, including coq au vin, osso bucco, cassoulet, and beef burgundy.

As a general proposition, there are really only two speeds at which food is cooked. Grilling and sautéing are fast techniques, while braising and baking are slow methods. Braising is the cooking of food either partially or totally immersed in liquid, which can be stock, wine, water, or some combination of these. Braising is

an effective method of rendering tougher cuts of meat more tender, as muscle requires long slow cooking. These cuts of meat, like shoulder or shanks, are the less expensive parts of the animal, as opposed to the more premium loin. This is peasant food, which requires long slow cooking before yielding a tender meal. When it is freezing outside, you are not likely to grill outdoors, and having the oven on for long time periods of time provides comfort as well as a meal.

It always helps to use stock when braising, but if that is not available water may be substituted, though the resulting sauce will not be as rich or full flavored. However, in the process of simmering meat slowly in liquid, you almost create your own stock. If the resulting sauce is too thin, it can always be thickened with flour or cornstarch, or better yet, reduced over heat to intensify and concentrate the flavor. The addition of a little tomato paste to beef dishes cooked in water will thicken the sauce and add intensity to the flavor. Wine also tenderizes muscle, and the classic preparations of coq au vin or beef burgundy rely heavily on the wine to flavor the sauce and soften the meat.

A heavy bottomed casserole is an ideal vessel for braising, and a secure lid is essential. The whole idea is to keep the liquid in, and if you attempt to cook something in liquid for a long time inside the oven without a lid, by the end of the process most of the liquid will have evaporated. Braising is a forgiving cooking technique, because unlike a roast, which can become overcooked and dry, there is little risk of this when braising. While it's true the something braised too long may tend to fall apart, it will still be tender and delicious. A stewed chicken is almost supposed to fall off the bone.

In my first professional cooking job in New York City many years ago, the restaurateur I worked for had one question he always asked upon hearing about a new dish I had prepared. "Is it juicy?" If it had been braised, the answer was surely yes.

Braised Pork with Black Beans & Cumin Seed (Serves 6)

Ingredients

1½ lb. pork butt, cut into small cubes

Flour seasoned with salt and pepper, for dredging

3 oz. slab bacon, cut in half-inch cubes

1 cup minced onion

2 green pepper, sliced into long strips

1 red pepper, sliced into long strips

2 carrots, diced

2 oz. minced garlic

½ t whole cumin seed

1 t ground cumin

Pinch crushed red pepper (optional)

1 bay leaf

2 t kosher salt

2 cups cooked black beans

3 cups peeled, diced tomato

1½ cups dry white wine

Directions

Preheat oven to 350°

1. Dredge the pork in seasoned flour and brown in sauté pan. Set aside.

2. In a heavy bottomed sauce pot, brown the bacon. When crisp, add the minced onion and cook over moderate heat for five minutes

3. Add the peppers, continue to stir and brown, then add the carrots and shallots.

4. Add the remaining ingredients.

5. Cover the pot and place in the oven for 2 hours.

6. Serve with rice and/or tortillas.

A Chicken in Every Pot

AT THE START of the last Great Depression almost a century ago, candidate Herbert Hoover promised both "a chicken in every pot and a car in every garage." The economy continues to fluctuate wildly, but the notion of having a chicken in every pot remains appealing. When Hoover made his promise, chicken was a luxury more expensive then beef. In 1930 a whole dressed chicken sold for $6.48 a pound, adjusted for inflation. Modern industrial agricultural practices have lowered the price to about $1.60 a pound today.

Although a huge portion of the world survives on a few grains of rice or beans, and only dreams of being able to eat a chicken, that is still something most Americans have no trouble affording. Over 30 years later I still recall the theory of social justice developed by an old high school history teacher. In the midst of the student anti-war rallies, the rise of the Black Panthers and The Weathermen, he announced that there would never be a

revolution in this country as long as most people could go home at night and have a chicken dinner. Thirty years later he remains correct. The Bolsheviks following Lenin and the guerrilla fighters supporting Fidel in the hills of Cuba no doubt were hungrier.

Certain types of food are archetypal, and exist in many different cultures.

Ravioli, pierogi, steamed dumplings are all variations on the same thing. Chicken in a pot is no different. Chicken stewed in a pot can be found in the cuisine of a wide variety of cultures: whether cooked in red wine as in coq au vin, or with tomatoes and vegetables like chicken cacciatore, or in a Mongolian hot pot with broth, noodles, and vegetables, or with red beans and rice, or perhaps curry and coconut milk and or tamarind, it seems to satisfy a primal urge. While grilling outside is an appealing way to cook in summer, in the cold dark months of winter, the bouquet of simmering food over a fire is what comforts us.

Unlike grilled or roasted chicken, it is hard to overcook chicken cooked in liquid. It might fall apart, but it will remain juicy and moist.

I remain hopelessly retro, and am attracted to those primal comforting meals that are so satisfying to me. We have lived through several periods of boom and bust over the past few decades, and since then countless jobs have disappeared. Never have we needed a chicken in every pot as much as we do now.

Braised Chicken with Lemon & Sage (Serves 4)

Ingredients

1 chicken (3½ pounds), cut into 8 pieces

flour seasoned with dried sage

vegetable oil

2 T finely minced shallots

1 t minced garlic

juice and zest of 2 lemons

3 T finely chopped fresh sage

1 cup diced carrots

3 cups chicken stock

Sage leaves for garnish

Directions

Preheat oven to 350°

1. Dredge the chicken in seasoned flour.

2. In a heavy bottomed sauce pot brown in vegetable oil for 3 minutes on each side.

2. Remove the chicken from the pan and add the shallots, garlic, and sage. Sauté for one minute, then add the carrots.

3. Return the chicken to the pan. Add the lemon juice, zest, and chicken stock.

4. Cover tightly and place the pan in the preheated oven for 25 minutes.

5. To serve, remove the chicken from the pan. Serve over orzo, risotto, couscous. Pour the sauce on top. Garnish with fresh sage leaves.

Cooking With and Without Heat

IN THE MIDST of a particularly cold Berkshire winter, when subzero temperatures and blustery winds have made going outside for even the briefest moment seem like an endurance test, it's an appropriate moment to reflect on the virtues and importance of cooking. Webster's Dictionary defines cooking as "preparing food for eating especially by means of heat." It is the application of heat to food that is a distinctly human achievement and one of the characteristics that distinguishes Homo sapiens from other animals. Other species gather berries and graze on grains, but we are the only ones who transform those raw ingredients with heat. Berries become pie, and wheat turns into bread. Grains of rice, which are inedible raw, become the most widespread staple when cooked. Perhaps nothing soothes the soul more on a frigid night than a bowl of hot broth or soup.

In light of the fundamental importance of cooking food, and transforming raw ingredients with heat, it is remarkable how popular two food trends have become, which involve no cooking at all. As little as a generation or two ago, Japanese restaurants that served sushi were few and far between in this country, but they

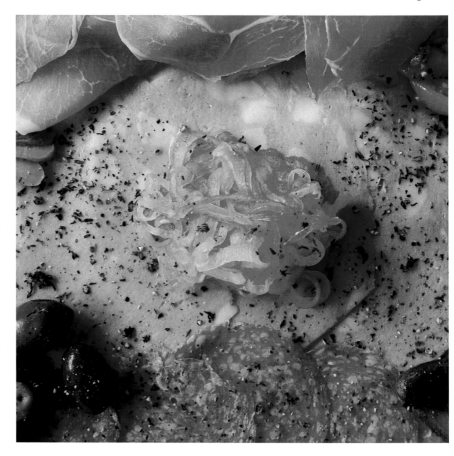

have become commonplace today. Just a generation ago, in the aftermath of Pearl Harbor, racist war propaganda sought to demonize the Japanese. With derogatory depictions of a culture of raw fish eaters, they were portrayed as the complete opposite of blue blooded Americans who ate steak and beef. Two generations later, many Americans have largely eliminated the consumption of beef from their diet, and embraced the consumption of raw fish. In an equally remarkable reversal of diet, the Japanese now consume record levels of beef. They are still the largest foreign importer of American beef, despite the first discovery of mad cow disease that caused the temporary suspension of imports.

Another food trend growing in popularity, particularly on the coasts and among the Hollywood set, is the raw food movement. The guiding principal behind this diet is the belief that once food is heated above the temperature of 118 degrees, valuable vitamins and nutrients are destroyed. In addition to being vegetarian, followers of the raw food diet mostly refrain from eating eggs and dairy products as well. One of the key food preparation techniques is the use of food dryers that eliminate the water in fruits and vegetables. Dried fruits and vegetables can be prepared in inventive and unusual ways in which their fresh versions cannot. Many of us are by now familiar with dried tomatoes, apples, bananas, and plums, all eaten dried and raw and often used to make salads. If you imagine that this regimen is simpler than cooking, consider just how much work is involved in sprouting seeds and air-drying fruits and vegetables.

Those of us more firmly rooted in traditional western cooking techniques may expand our culinary horizons to include uncooked food, but for most people, the application of fire will remain the essential part of the cooking process. While it is true that the chemical and physical process of cooking does destroy some nutrients, it is also true that cooking develops and brings out the flavors of many foods. As anyone who has eaten chocolate straight out of the refrigerator knows, flavors that are dull and muted on the palette when chilled are often more vibrant when warm or cooked. Other flavors that are harsh and overpowering when raw, like ginger

Pickled Red Onions (Serves 4)

Ingredients

2 red onions, peeled and sliced as thin as possible

1½ cups apple cider vinegar

¾ cup sugar

6 whole black peppercorns

1 bay leaf

Directions

1. Slice the onions as thinly as possible. A slicing machine is best if available. Place the onions in a small glass or stainless steel container.

2. Heat the vinegar until just short of boiling, add the sugar, and stir well.

3. Add the peppercorns and bay leaf.

4. Pour the hot vinegar mix over the onions, and let sit until cooked, about an hour.

5. Remove the bay leaf and peppercorns, and drain.

6. Serve chilled in a sandwich, with charcuterie items, or any sliced meat.

or garlic, become tamed and balanced when cooked. That reliance on temperature for optimum taste is the miracle of cooking, and what requires skill.

One technique that is somewhere in the middle is pickling, which is a great way to preserve food. Though the food is no longer raw, it's not like steaming, roasting, or grilling. It mostly involves marinating vegetables in heated vinegar, and is quite simple, and well within the grasp of just about anyone. This recipe for pickled red onions makes a great accompaniment for charcuterie, sliced meats, or a sandwich.

A Latke Went to Indonesia

DID YOU HEAR THE ONE about the latke that went to Indonesia? That's not a set up for a Borscht Belt joke; it's a shorthand explanation of a new dish we have been recently serving at the Café.

Like many other people, I have long been an inveterate lover of potato latkes. They are traditionally eaten during the winter and holiday season and not for the rest of the year but this leads me to how chefs should evolve and update menu ideas to create new dishes.

The idea of theme and variation is a very old one, particularly familiar to Classical musical composers. Bach wrote 32 Goldberg Variations on a single theme, Beethoven wrote 33 Diabelli Variations, and Brahms wrote a beautiful symphonic work based on a theme of Haydn. Those great musicians knew that they could take a kernel of a good idea, vary it, and create a completely new work.

Of course the obvious variation on a potato latke is to use a similar starchy vegetable like sweet potato or celery root. Both are indeed delicious, but not that much of a variation, and it doesn't really change the essential nature of the dish.

But what if a latke went to Indonesia? There it might be made of mung bean sprouts and scallions, and seasoned with ginger. Now that would be truly different. Indonesia is also the home to a very different variety of soy sauce, which is like molasses, and much thicker and sweeter than most other soy sauces. It is called *Kecap Manis* and is available in specialty food stores. It is one of my favorite exotic ingredients, though not very expensive.

The medium in which a latke is fried is almost as important as the ingredients it is made out of. One of the distinguishing features of Eastern European cuisine is the use of rendered poultry fat, or *schmaltz*, as a fat for frying. It is less commonly used today, especially in this country, but the aroma of onions and potatoes fried in *schmaltz* still evokes memories of an earlier time. Of course, rendered poultry is not to be found in Indonesian cuisine, but there the use of toasted sesame oil also imparts a characteristic aroma and taste.

As a lover of applesauce on potato latkes, I have always thought that latkes have an affinity for slightly sweet sauces, and this Indonesian soy sauce fits the bill perfectly. The resulting Ginger, Scallion and Mung Bean

---

Ginger, Scallion and Mung Bean Pancakes (Serves 6)

Ingredients

4 cups mung bean sprouts	2 T finely chopped ginger
2 T minced shallot	4 eggs
2 bunches finely chopped scallions	1/3 cup flour
1 red pepper, minced	toasted sesame oil for frying

Directions

1. Chop the Mung beans coarsely and place in mixing bowl.

2. Add the remaining ingredients, and mix well.

3. Heat some sesame oil in a skillet until very hot, and fry about 3 tablespoons of pancake mix.

4. Use a spoon to flatten out the pancake as thin as possible, and cook for 2 minutes on each side.

5. Serve with a drizzle of Kecap Manis sweet soy sauce, and garnish with more scallions.

Pancake is a delicious vegetarian appetizer, even though my grandmother probably wouldn't recognize the genesis of the idea.

A Piece of Cake

"**A** PIECE OF CAKE." That's what we say when we mean something is easy. It's true, eating a piece of cake is a piece of cake. However, making one is another matter. Although it is not terribly challenging to make a cake, the mere fact that it requires turning on an oven, separating eggs, and using an electric mixer means that it is not something most home cooks attempt very often. If you want a good cake, you're probably going to have to make it yourself. What is for sale in the bakery department of your local supermarket is made with a collection of artificial flavors, chemical emulsifiers and stabilizers, and is scarcely edible. A box cake isn't much better.

We save cakes for important events, prominent and almost required on two of our most cherished occasions: birthdays and weddings. Yes, there is an occasional birthday pie, and of late cupcakes have become a hot trend for weddings, but for the most part weddings and birthdays call for cake. Wedding cakes have a deservedly bad reputation, since many are frosted with shortening, instead of using real butter or cream. You can spot a cake frosted with shortening from afar; they have an unnatural white color, and a slightly unyielding hardness to them. Shortening is good for frying chicken in, but you really don't want to eat it slathered all over your cake.

As a child growing up I still have fond memories of licking the beaters from my mother's Kitchen Aid electric mixer. Today's food police would never allow that anymore, given the widespread alarm over salmonella. The tradition in my family was that my mother made our favorite cake on our birthday. My eldest brother wanted strawberry shortcake, another brother and sister picked chocolate cake, and of course, blueberry pie for my father. They are all worthy contenders, and delicious, but they are not what *I* want on *my* birthday.

The origin of my favorite cake, and how it came to be named, is unclear. It goes back a generation to my father's bookkeeper, who was an excellent baker.

Alice was a plump woman and a great baker, and she frequently brought in plates of goodies into the office. She was one of those people who seemed to derive great pleasure from watching other people devour her handiwork, and my father and his employees were only too happy to oblige. She had a particular affinity for coffee cakes. Though she passed away many years ago, her spirit and legacy live on in many favorite recipes.

Some people are secretive about recipes, and afraid to reveal the magic. I, however, like Alice, have always been in favor of spreading the knowledge. Recipes are part of the family legacy that gets transmitted from one generation to the next, and as such, should be treasured. Like old black and white photos and family picture albums, dog-eared index cards with favorite recipes are part of our heritage, and should be passed on to family and friends. To lose a recipe is to lose a part of history.

While I pass along this recipe to you, and have had its authenticity and accuracy vouched for, I am happy to report that I have never had to make it myself. Birthday cakes, by definition, are made *for* you and this is one dish I don't make. The more people who know how to make my favorite cake, the more likely it will be made for me on my birthday. In difficult times, it's comforting to know that there is a hunk of such a gift in my freezer.

My birthday cake has always been called, I am embarrassed to say, *He-Man Cake*. I don't know why it is called that, but I can't imagine referring to it any other way. Of course one would never choose that name today, and one needn't be either strong or virile to make or eat it. It is a simple, rich, and basic cake, and He-Man cake is equally beloved by both men and women. It is further graced by the additional virtue possessed by some coffee cakes of actually being better the second day, assuming you can resist eating the whole thing on the first one.

He-Man Cake (Serves 8-10)

Ingredients

Cake:
4 egg whites
½ lb. butter
2 cups sugar
4 egg yolks
1 cup milk
2 ½ cups flour
2 ½ t baking powder

1 t vanilla
¼ t salt

Topping:
⅓ cup melted butter
⅓ cup sugar
3 t cinnamon
1 ½ cups chopped
   walnuts

Directions

1. Preheat oven to 350°

2. Grease a 10" tube pan with a removable center while oven is preheating.

3. Warm the egg whites, beat into soft peaks, and set aside.

4. Cream the butter, sugar and egg yolks in a mixer.

5. Add the rest of the ingredients, alternately.

6. Fold the beaten egg whites into the mixture.

7. Pour the batter into the pan.

8. Combine the topping ingredients and spoon over the top of the batter.

9. Bake for 1¼-1½ hours. Let cake cool for several hours before trying to invert the cake from the pan.

He-Man cake needs no icing, though a cup of coffee or a slab of ice cream make a nice accompaniment. The recipe follows. It's a piece of cake.

Grand Finale

I'T'S AN OLD TRUISM in show business that it's important to end with a Grand Finale. Everyone from Beethoven to Tchaikovsky to Broadway musicals and firework operators know how important it is to leave guests with a memorable ending and a smile on their face. It is just as true in the restaurant and catering business, particularly true for those gala dinners that fill the Berkshire social calendar.

The five or six month cultural season in the Berkshires is high season for festive dinners. Nearly every arts and nonprofit organization plans some kind of fundraising event or dinner, and on any given weekend

there are multiple events taking place, most involving food. These dinners were once disparagingly referred to by some as "rubber chicken dinners," because the food was boring and tasteless. But that need not be the case, and it is certainly less true today than it was years ago.

When the organizers of the *Berkshire International Film Festival* asked me to cater a dinner for 100 or more guests, I wanted to devise a menu that was delicious. Not only was the taste important but it also needed to be one that could be easily served, and included a memorable dessert.

We had been serving a rich and savory tomato soup seasoned with smoked Gouda cheese, and that was chosen as the first course. For our main course, I chose a variety of special occasion dishes. A bit retro and old fashioned, Surf and Turf is having a resurgence of popularity, and is a great choice because it satisfies both carnivores and fish eaters. It also works out nicely because it can be served at room temperature and holds up well if dinner is delayed, or guests choose to stand and chat rather than sit down and eat.

Catering also demands a certain flexibility, and ability to roll with the punches. As the Film Festival opening approached, the weather forecast was for unusually hot and sticky weather in the Berkshires, after an unpleasantly chilly and rainy spring. The hot soup that had earlier seemed appealing was clearly the wrong choice in 90 degree weather, and the obvious choice was to substitute salad. Now with salad and Surf and Turf on the menu, the last step was the dessert.

Months earlier I was walking through the aisles of *Guido's* when I spied a whole coconut, and I got the idea of cutting it in half, and stuffing the middle with some berries.

I wasn't sure how to cut a coconut in half, and trim off the ends so they would stand up on the plate and still have 10 fingers in the end. I approached Jim Law of *Under Mountain Joiners*, who experimented cutting some, after which we knew it would work. Chefs often cite farmers, wine makers, bakers, and foragers for their menu success, but it's not often that a woodworker is credited.

When filled with SoCo mango sorbet, drizzled with raspberry and mango sauces, showered with toasted coconut and fresh berries, garnished with fresh mint, a rolled Gaufrette cookie and a chocolate covered macaroon, a half coconut does indeed make for a Grand Finale.

PART III

Food Trends

· · · · · · · · · · · · · · · · · · ·

Farmers, Foragers and Deconstruction

TWO VERY DIFFERENT PHILOSOPHIES of cooking prevail today, and they couldn't be more different. The first is the Farm to Table movement with its focus on using local and sustainably produced foods, and the other is known as molecular deconstruction (their name, not mine), which seeks to alter some of the basic physical properties of food. Clearly the Berkshires are very much in the vanguard of the Farm to Table movement, and one would have to travel to Europe or major urban areas in this country to find molecular deconstruction.

Styles of painting and music change over time, and so does cooking. No one writes music in the style of Bach or Mozart anymore, no one still paints in the style of Rembrandt or the French Impressionists, and there aren't many restaurants that cook traditional French cuisine today. Classical French cuisine was an outgrowth of the French Revolution, yet its influence and dominance continued until after the Second World War. Modern restaurants began at the end of the 1700's, and the repertoire of basic sauces and styles of cuisine date to this era. Recipes and techniques were developed, standardized, and strictly defined. Like Olympic figure skating, a chef was judged on how well he executed these dishes, and creativity was not prized.

The social revolutions sweeping the world in the 60's wasn't limited to sex, drugs, and rock and roll. The same impulse to question authority, experiment, and defy rules was felt in kitchens. There was a rebellion against the older style, which didn't allow for creativity, and which featured heavy sauces, sauces thickened with flour, and food plated in the dining room by captains and waiters. The hallmark of *nouvelle cuisine*, as it became to be known, was a lighter style of eating. Rich, cream-based sauces were replaced by sauces made from vegetable purees, and simpler preparations were favored over complicated ones. Chefs became known for their individual styles and distinctive dishes, not for merely reproducing the classical repertoire. The legacy of this revolution is still very much with us today.

Prior to the turn of the 20th century, chefs had no choice but to use locally raised organic ingredients, because there were no other kinds. But with the emergence of modern industrial agriculture in the post war period, some began to recognize the poor quality food grown with massive chemical inputs and shipped across the country. When Alice Waters opened *Chez Panisse* in 1971, she was just looking for the vegetables that tasted best, which is how she discovered organic vegetables.

The organic vegetable movement led in part to the founding of the first Community Supported Agriculture (CSA) Farm, in Great Barrington, Massachusetts in 1986. These farms united growers and buyers into a compact. Shortly afterwards *Berkshire Grown* was founded. The mission of *Berkshire Grown* is to help farmers and chefs communicate and do business together, and the results can be seen on the menus of dozens of the county's restaurants, which prominently feature local farm products. Thirty years later there are now 35 CSAs in the county, and 146 farms who partner in Berkshire Grown, growing and producing the entire range of food. Chefs in the Berkshires have an ever-increasing harvest of bounty to incorporate into their menus, and this has become the defining characteristic of cooking in the Berkshires.

Every revolution has a counter-revolution, and while some chefs were interested in preserving traditional agriculture and getting back to the farm, another group of chefs has been influenced and fascinated by the increasing role of technology in the world. Led by renowned Spanish Chef Ferran Adrià, there is a generation of chefs growing up who take their inspiration more from the chemistry lab than the farm, and who are more interested in manipulating the physical properties of ingredients in novel ways, than in faithfully recreating the cuisine of their culture.

The current rage among disciples of revolutionary Chef Adrià, is to "molecularly deconstruct" food. That's the term they use to refer to what they do — not "cooking." Adrià is clearly the most prominent chef associated with this movement, but he has many disciples throughout the world. He defines his approach as "taking a dish that is well known and transforming all its ingredients, or part of them; then modifying the dish's texture, form and/or its temperature. Deconstructed, such a dish will preserve its essence... but its appearance will be radically different from the original's. In their hands, parts of a chicken might be flash frozen with liquid nitrogen, ground up, and turned into a powder, while other parts might be made into foam, while still other pieces might be combined with gelatin and turned into a noodle.

Nor would he preclude using chicken in dessert. In the end you might not recognize anything you were eating as chicken.

Adrià's restaurant is closed now, but used to only be open to the public for six months a year, and he used the rest of the year to retreat to his test kitchen to create new "mad scientist" cuisine. The source of his inspiration was the laboratory, where culinary experiments were conducted and perfected.

Some of the dishes from Adrià's repertoire include frozen whisky sour candy, white garlic and almond sorbet, tobacco-flavored blackberry crushed ice and Kellogg's paella (Rice Krispies, shrimp heads and vanilla-flavored mashed potatoes).

This style of cooking is impossible without using modern thickening agents, sugar substitutes, enzymes, liquid nitrogen, dehydration and other nontraditional means. The recipes call for chemical stabilizers and additives, including sodium alginate, xanthan gum, glycerin flakes, kappa carrageenan, and hydroxypropyl methylcellulose. All these ingredients are safe to eat — but they are scarcely ingredients obtained from the local farmer.

Run fast when you see the word deconstruction applied to food.

In the Berkshires, there are few chefs deconstructing food. We search out the highest quality farm products, and use them in authentic ways that honor the integrity of the ingredients. Most of us are also buying locally to ensure the survival of local farms, and willing to pay a premium for the high quality. Many of our diners understand that grass fed beef and local organic vegetables cost more than industrially grown food — and that is exactly why they come to the Berkshires to dine.

Gluten Free Dining

RESTAURANTS that don't change with the times close and go out of business. Tastes and styles change, and what was once cutting edge and popular can become passé and archaic. You have to search hard now to find restaurants that serve some of the old classics of French cuisine, like Beef Wellington and Veal Oscar. The clientele that grew up eating that food has largely passed away, as did many of the restaurants that featured that kind of menu. They have been replaced by diners who avoid cream and carbohydrates. In the age of high cholesterol, a lot of people find Hollandaise sauce unappealing and unhealthy, and except for an occasional appearance on Eggs Benedict at brunch, it has been relegated to the cuisine of yesteryear. Few restaurants flambé desserts tableside anymore, or prepare anything at all at the table, though that was once regarded as elegant and sophisticated.

While it was once enough to just list steak on the menu, discerning customers now want to know if it is local and/or grass fed. Meat can't be anonymous anymore; diners want to know the provenance or the name of the farm, as they rightly should. Accordingly, the menu at Castle Street features locally raised grass fed beef from *Ioka Valley Farm*, and *North Plain Farm* pork.

Ever since the protein craze based on the Atkins diet, a substantial part of the dining public avoids carbohydrates. Restaurants had to respond to requests to eliminate carbohydrates from their plate. We get orders all the time for burgers without the bun or fries, and with a salad or vegetables instead. This is the hospitality business, so we are happy to accommodate special requests.

After many years of answering questions about which menu items are gluten free and which aren't, we now indicate that on the menu. Increasing numbers of diners are looking for gluten free food, and it's important to honor special orders, as well as provide assurance to both wait staff and diners about the ingredients in the food. The irony is that most of the menu has always been gluten free, not by design, but because grilled and sautéed meat, fish, and poultry with vegetables are simply gluten free by themselves. It's an amazingly simple request to honor and fulfill, but many diners tell me of unfortunate encounters in other restaurants, where they had a hard time getting what they wanted, or being understood. These people have thanked us for indicat-

---

Grilled Swordfish with Mango and Mint Salsa (Serves 4)

Four 6-8 oz. swordfish filets

Brush the swordfish filets with oil and grill for about 2 minutes on each side. Be careful not to overcook. Serve with a dollop of Mango & Mint Salsa.

Combine all ingredients and mix well.

Mango & Mint Salsa

1 mango, peeled and diced	1 T finely minced red onion
2 T finely chopped mint	½ t honey
2 T finely chopped cilantro	1 t rice wine vinegar
Juice and zest of one lime	3 T vegetable oil

ing which items on the menu are gluten free, and which can be adjusted to be gluten free. For instance, French Onion soup without the crouton is gluten free, and simple to make. A year or two ago I didn't think this was important enough to mark on the menu, but I do now. Times change, and so have we.

Grilled fish has always been gluten free and is delicious.

Farmer's Market Menu Planning

SUMMERTIME in the Berkshire-Taconic area means that for a few brief months we are liberated from shopping indoors in enclosed markets and are able to shop at several area farmers' markets. For much of the year we indulge ourselves with raspberries flown in from Guatemala and asparagus from Chile. But for the three to four months of summer, these and other fresh farm products are available for sale directly from the farmer at several area weekly outdoor farmers' markets. Many of us who eat food shipped in from unknown origins rejoice at the idea of being able to know who grew our food, at least during the summer season.

Shopping at a farmer's market is different from shopping at a large indoor market. For starters, most people selling the food actually grew it, rather than merely put in packages. Shopping at the farmer's market means having the opportunity to buy and eat food that was often literally picked that morning, instead of a week

ago before beginning a truck ride across America.

Rather than arriving at a farmer's market with a list of desired purchases, it is perhaps more in keeping with the spirit of the place to be open to surprises and see what looks freshest and most appealing. Instead of deciding the evening's menu before you arrive, allow the serendipity of the garden's harvest to decide your menu.

Never had a fried squash blossom? They only have the briefest season, and it would be a shame not to take advantage of their availability in the market. Is there a table with extraordinary little miniature patty pan squash? They make a delicious first course when scooped out like a pumpkin and stuffed with a vegetable or couscous filling. Is someone offering slightly bruised eggplant or zucchini at a discount? It's time to whip up a batch of ratatouille.

We New Englanders know from the Gershwin line that living easy in summertime is an all too passing a phenomena, but it is our reward for enduring blizzards and seemingly interminable bleak days. Farmer's markets are a celebration of easy living. You can buy strawberries all year long in the supermarket, but because the difference is so enormous, I would never think of making strawberry shortcake with anything but the best locally grown berries. The season for local strawberries in the Berkshires is at best two weeks, so you had better strike while the iron is hot.

Old Fashioned Shortcake with Berries

Shortcake is really just a form of biscuit, made with baking powder. They are easy to make, and best if the dough is not handled too much. You don't even really need a rolling pin to make these, just use the base of your hand to flatten out the dough on the work table.

Old Fashioned Shortcake with Berries (Serves 4)

Ingredients

Shortcake:
1¾ cup sifted flour
2½ teaspoons baking powder
1 t salt
1 T sugar

⅛ cup butter
¾ cup milk

Topping:
Fresh berries
Whipped cream

Directions

1. Preheat oven to 450°

2. Combine the flour, salt, sugar, and baking powder, and mix well.

3. Cut in the butter, and use your fingers to break it up into small pieces.

4. Add the milk, and mix with a spoon.

5. Combine the dough into a ball, and without over handling, flatten it out on a table coated with flour, until the dough is about ¾" thick. Use a biscuit cutter or glass to cut the biscuit into rounds.

6. Place the biscuits on a parchment paper lined baking pan, and bake in preheated oven for 10 minutes, until golden brown.

7. Allow the biscuits to cool, and then cut in half like an English muffin, and fill the middle with whipped cream and mixed fresh berries. Replace the top on the biscuit, and add more whipped cream and fresh berries. Serve with raspberry sauce.

If you don't have a biscuit cutter, a large round glass can be used to cut out the biscuits.

Is Fusion Confusion?

ON THE OCCASION of the celebration of 25 years in business, the renowned French Chef Alain Ducasse invited a collection of some the world's leading chefs to a dinner in Monaco at his famed Le Louis XV restaurant. In the course of an interview, Ducasse reaffirmed his belief that French training and French tradition remain the foundation of haute cuisine all over the world. But Chef Ducasse went even further, pronouncing that in his opinion, "fusion is confusion."

It's such a pithy and elegant quote that it deserves further scrutiny. Having just returned from Paris where I dined at *Benoit*, his 2 star traditional bistro, his comments caught my attention. Ducasse is in a league of his own and when he speaks, it is with the voice of authority. He is the first chef to receive 3 Michelin stars in 3 different restaurants, and collectively he is one of only two chefs to garner 21 Michelin stars.

Like Tevye in *Fiddler on the Roof*, I am one who appreciates and respects Tradition. I am very fond of not only the classic dishes of French Cuisine, but also those techniques. At the Café we make stocks, which translated in French as *fonds* are the very foundation of the cuisine. We regularly feature such dishes as cassoulet, coq au vin, bouillabaisse, and steak au poivre, which are immediately recognizable to Francophiles all over the world. I don't want anyone messing around with classics just for the sake of being cutting edge.

Yet the world is changing, and even those most determined to hang on to old traditions can't help but recognize that it's harder to be a purist in a world where information and ingredients travel so quickly. We have come a long way from the time when chefs rarely ventured beyond their small village, and cooks worked only with traditional ingredients gathered nearby. Haute cuisine was developed and codified during the 19th century as almost a sacred doctrine and an expression of medieval fealty to tradition, not allowing for or recognizing improvisation or innovation. But we now live in an age when authority and tradition are questioned and challenged, and not just blindly followed. Few 19th century French chefs were exposed to diverse ingredients like couscous, wasabi, cilantro, maple syrup, sesame oil, or lemongrass, but these ingredients have now become commonplace. Today, inventive and curious chefs are tempted to combine these ingredients in ways never imagined by their predecessors. These new dishes may not be the haute cuisine classics that Ducasse knows, but they can be delicious nonetheless. The trick is to distinguish between ideas that work and are well considered, and those that are mere attempts to gain attention by going where no chef has ever gone before…and shouldn't.

One can't help but be influenced by the enormous exposure to information from other dining experiences, TV, and the Internet. Ducasse's grandparents may not have known much about Asian and North African cuisine, but Ducasse's kitchens are no doubt staffed in part by immigrants from those regions who bring a different take to French cuisine.

There is no shortage of the ultra-wealthy to patronize Ducasse's expensive restaurants. Yet somehow haute French cuisine simply seems less relevant in a world where diners can chose among an extraordinary array of the world's cuisines, most of which are served in a less formal manner, and at a much lower price. Even

among those who can afford to frequently dine in his kind of restaurant, many choose to dine more casually, less expensively, and less calorically. The butter, foie gras, and truffles that are featured so prominently in haute cuisine are too rich for the palette of many younger eaters, and fewer diners want to dress in the manner required for this style of restaurant.

Inexorably connected to the kind of haute cuisine Ducasse serves are the great wines of Bordeaux and Burgundy, and here too the world has experienced a huge change in little more than a generation. The classified wines of France, which are featured on the wine lists of these restaurants, have reached stratospheric prices, while New World wines from America, South America, Australia and New Zealand offer a real alternative at an enormous discount. Those wines simply didn't exist a generation ago, but they do now, and they are changing the way we eat. The wine in my coq au vin is more likely to be New World Syrah or Cabernet rather than Bordeaux, and it represents a kind of fusion unthinkable just a short time ago.

The following recipe is an example of fusion cuisine that I find perfectly delicious, if not haute cuisine. In Normandy the French serve fish or chicken with apples and cream, and this variation using coconut milk is but a variation on that theme. I hope Chef Ducasse would not find this confusing.

Sea Scallops with Macoun Apples and Coconut Milk

The following recipe is the result of a bit of serendipity at a local farm stand. I had been purchasing apples with the intent of making applesauce when the thought of combining sautéed sea scallops with apples struck me. Macoun apples are slightly sweet and firm, and work well in this recipe. The influences in this recipe are both New England and South Asian, and the blend of ginger, apples, and coconut milk is typical of much of the fusion cuisine of recent years. The richness of the coconut milk is more appealing in the cooler weather, and the addition of a few chilies will also help keep you warm. *Bon Appetit!*

Sea Scallops with Macoun Apples and Coconut Milk (Serves 4)

Ingredients

1 ½ lbs. dry sea scallops

1 t minced shallots

1 t minced fresh ginger

¼ t curry powder (optional)

1 red pepper, julienned

Dash crushed red pepper flakes

2 Macoun apples, thinly sliced

4 oz. canned coconut milk

1 T black currants

Directions

1. Clean the scallops by removing and discarding the tough muscle on the side.

2. Heat a large skillet with a little vegetable oil, and add the shallots, scallops, ginger, optional curry, julienned red pepper, crushed red pepper, and the apples.

3. Stir well for about 2-3 minutes, and then add the coconut milk. Continue to cook for another minute while stirring well, allowing the coconut milk to reduce.

4. Divide among 4 plates, served over rice and garnished with dried black currants.

Radical & Conservative

IN REFERENCE TO BOTH our politics and our gastronomy, the labels radical and conservative have been tossed about with increasing abandon, and the words have come to lose their meaning. A previous president lost the popular election but won the Supreme Court appointment, desecrated the Bill of Rights, invaded a country that didn't attack us, and pursued environmental policies designed to foster irreversible climate change, but was considered conservative. Meanwhile, President Obama, the most centrist in a generation, is accused of being a Socialist.

To review the dictionary definition, the root of the word conservative is to preserve, which implies valuing and holding on to the past. Radical means an extreme departure from usual and normal traditions.

We live in a time of such enormous and rapid change, that it is hard to keep perspective. Like Einstein's examination of passengers on two separate moving trains, it is sometimes difficult to determine which train is moving, and if so, in which direction.

When it comes to how and what we eat, who are the real radicals today? At the turn of the last century, the vast majority of Americans lived on farms and produced at least some of

their own food. That is no longer true. Americans spend the majority of their total food dollars on prepared food or food eaten outside the home, and most of the grain, beef, and poultry processed and distributed in this country is controlled by a small handful of giant agribusinesses.

The robber barons of the 19th century who created this country's first industrial wealth did so largely through a combination of monopoly, intimidation, and lack of government regulation. But at least the Carnegies, Rockefellers and Mellons had a sense of noblesse oblige and stewardship, and they also left a legacy of libraries, land conservation, and universities. That is

almost entirely absent in today's global corporate world of Monsanto, McDonald's, and Cargill.

The food writer Michael Pollan has written that the single most radical thing anyone can do in America today is to grow some of his or her own food. In the popular culture, those who shop at food co-ops and farmers' markets are somehow depicted as Birkenstock-wearing hippies, Flower Children, or their descendents. Yet I submit that the impulse to try to preserve some element of the agrarian ideal is not radical at all, but rather deeply conservative, in the true dictionary meaning of the word. A wide range of writers, chefs, and activists, including Mr. Pollan, Frances Moore Lappé, and our own Berkshire Locavore Amy Cotler, recognize how critical it is to retain some control over the food supply.

So who are the real radicals? Is it those seed companies who patent life and deny farmers their age-old heritage, or industrial confined feeding operations with their gigantic manure lagoons? Perhaps it's those food companies who increasingly turn food into manufactured imitation food products, primarily through the addition of salt, fats, sugar, and unpronounceable chemicals?

After a long winter of cold and ice, we yearn for the first sign of green. Among the first crops out of the ground are both spinach and asparagus, and this recipe for Spinach and Asparagus Timbale makes use of each. It is perfect accompanied by fish or chicken.

Spinach and Asparagus Timbale

Timbales are round or oval shaped molds that are used to make a variety of vegetable puree accompaniments. They fall somewhere between a vegetable soufflé and a quiche, and make an unusual and colorful vegetable side dish that can be served with either fish or meat. Unlike a soufflé, which depends on beaten egg whites, timbales combine a vegetable puree with eggs and cream to make a rich vegetable pudding. They are baked in small molds that sit in a pan surrounded by water, and are cooked at low temperatures. *Bon Appetit!*

Spinach and Asparagus Timbale (Serves 6)

Ingredients

1 lb. spinach

6 eggs

1 cup heavy cream

1 bunch chopped fresh dill

½ cup diced asparagus

Salt and pepper

Directions

1. Preheat oven to 300°

2. Remove the stems from the spinach, and place the cleaned, washed leaves in a saucepot with ¼ cup of water, and steam for about 2 minutes in a covered pot.

3. Remove the spinach from the pot, rinse in cold water, and drain as much of the excess water from the spinach as possible.

4. Puree the spinach in a blender with the eggs.

5. Combine the spinach and egg puree with the heavy cream, dill, diced asparagus, and salt and pepper. Mix well.

6. Lightly grease the timbales molds (ceramic ramekins may be used), and fill them with the vegetable mix.

7. Place the timbales in a pan filled with water, and bake in preheated oven for about 40 minutes. Remove from the oven, unmold, and serve with fish or meat.

Timing is Everything

TIMING IS EVERYTHING, whether in investing, athletic competition, or many other affairs. Those who shorted the market, suspecting the real estate bubble wasn't sustainable, made a killing. Those who didn't lost homes and fortunes. The slight delay in moving to one side or the other by a shortstop, point guard, or running back can determine the outcome of a game or championship series.

There may be no realm in which the truth of this well-known adage is more evident than in cooking and eating. Certain cooking techniques like braising or poaching are very forgiving, and a few minutes of extra cooking doesn't make much difference. However, a thin steak or chop can be rendered dry or just slightly overcooked if it isn't removed from the skillet at just the right time. The best method for serving meat is to cook it until it is very rare, than wrap it tightly in foil, and let it rest for about 15 minutes before serving. The juices will set, and the meat will continue to cook slightly, but still be quite pink. But if left to sit too long, it will end up being overcooked.

The difference between perfectly moist gooey brownies, and ones that are dry and crumbly, is just a matter of minutes. Classic risotto should have a slight bite and chewiness, but when cooked too long it becomes as soft as oatmeal, and not nearly as satisfying. In a matter of minutes pasta can go from cooked perfectly al dente, to overcooked and mushy.

Perhaps even more than in cooking techniques, timing is critical in selecting what to cook and eat. It is not how you cook, but what you choose to eat in the first place that is so important. Real tomatoes are available for about six weeks a year in the Berkshires, and that is the only time I would consider trying to make gazpacho, or serving fresh mozzarella and tomatoes. While

the latter is a beloved and classic dish, it only works if the tomatoes are great, and that is for but a few weeks a year. Really juicy melons are likewise harvested for a few weeks in late summer, after which the supermarket varieties are hardly worth eating. Nor is critical timing limited to just produce. The season for shad roe and soft shell crab is just a few weeks long, which is why they are so special, and expensive. The same is true for striped bass — one of my favorite fish to eat. The season is highly regulated, and the catch is limited to a month or two in the summer on the Atlantic Coast — and then you have to wait until next year.

One of the rarest delicacies of the summer season is squash blossoms. For a few weeks in early summer, before the vegetable itself grows, beautiful yellow flowers bloom on the plants. They can grow quite large — up to six inches long. They are very delicate, break easily, don't travel well, and begin to wilt after just a day or two. They are the kind of food you really do have to eat locally and know a farmer to get. You won't see squash blossoms on the shelf in the supermarket. Some people like to stuff them but I like them best deep fried. Serve them with a light Vietnamese style dipping sauce, which is as delicate as the fried flower. Squash blossoms aren't around for long, so grab them while you can.

Beer Battered Fried Squash Blossoms

Ingredients

6 large squash blossoms	6 oz. beer
1½ cups flour	1 t baking powder
1 cup cornmeal	Pinch salt
	Pinch cayenne pepper

Directions

1. Heat 2 quarts vegetable oil to 350° in a deep pot.

2. Mix all the dry ingredients together in a mixing bowl.

3. Add the beer, and stir well.

4. Carefully dunk and swirl the flowers in the beer batter, and shake off any excess.

5. Drop the flower in the oil, and cook for 2-3 minutes, depending on the size.

6. Remove the fried blossoms from the oil, drain well, and serve with the following dipping sauce

Vietnamese Style Dipping Sauce (Nuoc Cham)

Ingredients

3 T sugar	¼ cup finely shredded raw carrot
½ cup warm water	1 clove garlic, finely minced (optional)
3 T lime juice	2 T finely chopped cilantro
¼ cup fish sauce	
¼ cup scallion, finely chopped	

Directions

1. Combine fish sauce, water, sugar and lime juice in a small bowl and mix well until sugar is completely dissolved.

2. Add garlic, scallions, shredded carrot, and cilantro, and stir.

Vegetable Chic

ALL VEGETABLES may be created equal, but we humans who eat them certainly don't regard them that way. There are the "cool" and "in" vegetables, and then there are others, largely ignored, forgotten, and underutilized. We all know which vegetables belong in the first category. The ubiquitous mesclun and micro salad greens, thin spears of asparagus that are a harbinger of spring, ripe tomatoes from our gardens, fresh corn, and sugar snap peas are the vegetables with status that appear prominently on restaurant menus and in our own shopping baskets. To a large extent these are the vegetables we associate with the prime of spring and summer.

Many of the vegetables that are decidedly "uncool" are the vegetables we associate with fall and winter, and which many home cooks largely ignore. Among these vegetables are root vegetables like beets, celery root and parsnips, gourds and winter squash, the cabbage family, and the sturdy leafy vegetables like kale, chard, and turnip greens. In a kind of reverse chic, these vegetables are frequently encountered on the menus

of upscale restaurants, and rarely eaten at home. But as the temperature falls outside, and both chefs and diners are drawn to heartier eating, these are precisely the vegetables that deserve our attention. In addition, these are among the healthiest of all vegetables to eat and what nutritionists urge us to include in our diets, but which very few of us actually do. These vegetables require some vegetable affirmative action, to induce us to eat them more often. While we all know what broccoli looks like, how many people could identify the difference between a parsnip and a rutabaga?

The current carbophobia that is sweeping the nation makes it a little tougher to extol the virtues of celery root, but it is among my favorite fall vegetables. It is admittedly among the least attractive of all vegetables, and you must get past its gnarly exterior. Celery root can be used in virtually the same way as potatoes, but their intense, earthy flavor is unique and somehow comforting. Parsnips, which look like white carrots, also have a pronounced and distinctive flavor, and when roasted with a little butter, become slightly caramelized. For some reason borscht is much more commonly eaten chilled, but in the winter, a hot beet soup simmered with some beef, almost makes a complete meal.

Except for an appearance in coleslaw, cabbage is pretty much ignored in this country. While Mediterranean, Asian fusion, and Tex-Mex cuisines have flourished in this country in the past generation, Central and Middle European cuisine, which includes a lot of cabbage, has not been among the hot trends. This is a shame, because cabbage is nutritious, low in calories, and extremely savory. Chicken served with braised cabbage and shiitake mushrooms, and breast of duck with red cabbage and bacon, are just two of the delicious dishes made with cabbage that have appeared on the menu, and that can easily be made at home.

In less than a generation kale has gone from being one of the least commonly eaten vegetables in this country to one that is now so trendy it is the butt of jokes. It's the perfect accompaniment to duck confit, as it cuts through the fattiness of the duck. Since kale grows locally through late in the fall, it is timed perfectly with the arrival of duck confit on fall menus.

These vegetables tend to require a little more cooking time than a quick steam or sauté, but as the winter approaches and we spend more time cooking, they can provide a welcome change of pace. They may even become chic.

Swiss Chard and Goat Cheese Soufflé

(Makes one 9" pie pan, or 8 small soufflé cups)

Ingredients

1 lb. swiss chard (or spinach)

1 onion, sautéed

6 eggs

1 cup goat cheese

Pinch fresh thyme

1 t caraway or dill seeds

Salt and pepper

Directions

1. Preheat oven to 350°

2. Wash chard well, discard thick stems, and coarsely chop.

3. Mince the onion, and sauté until golden brown.

4. Separate the eggs.

5. Combine the chopped chard, sautéed onion, yolks, cheese and seasonings. Mix well.

6. Beat the whites until soft peaks form, and fold into mix.

7. Cook in well-greased ramekins or pie dish, about 30 minutes for pie dish, less time for smaller ramekins.

Timeless Classics and Old Warhorses

WHAT IS THE DIFFERENCE between a timeless classic and a tired old warhorse? It isn't only chefs who ask themselves that question. Along with restaurateurs, those who program symphonies and theaters are in the business of striking a balance between tradition and innovation. As we all know, Beethoven and Mozart continue to draw big crowds to Tanglewood, while electronic and contemporary music often plays to less than a full house. Yet the orchestral repertoire didn't end in the 18th or 19th or even 20th century. If the musical tradition is to stay alive, the works of living composers must be performed as well. The music of Stravinsky almost caused riots when first performed, but it is now safely established as part of the standard repertoire today. A lot can change in a generation or two.

The same issues face chefs and restaurateurs every day. Tried and true favorites can be popular, but if never varied or alternated with newer dishes, menus risk becoming boring and stodgy. I never cease to be amazed by the high percentage of customers who order the same thing every time they come for dinner. They're in the mood for a certain dish, they have an expectation about how it will taste, and it either lives up to their expectation, or they are disappointed. At the same time, other people arrive in the Café, and the first question they ask is: "What's new on the menu?" They want to be challenged by something they haven't eaten

before. The trick is to be able to accommodate both types of customers.

The past generation has seen a revolution in the way that a small group of tech-savvy chefs prepare food with "molecular deconstruction." Diners may struggle to figure out what it is that has been served on their plate when some of these concoctions come out. In the same way that some listeners don't regard atonal computer generated sound as being music, some diners may not think food that features ingredients that have been physically manipulated as being cuisine. There is indeed an audience for this kind of food, but perhaps just a limited one.

There are some dishes we simply can't take off the menu. We have been serving them since Day One, and there might be a popular insurrection if they were taken off the menu. The following is a variation on Puttanesca Sauce, which normally contains anchovies. I leave out the anchovies in order to keep the dish vegetarian, which is a consideration chefs a generation ago might not have weighed. As much as I like fresh tomatoes in season, some pasta dishes are actually better when made with high-quality canned tomatoes, which have been peeled and diced.

Because this sauce requires no cooking, it retains a fresh and lively taste. We call this Provençale Sauce. Just heat and toss with pasta.

Pasta Provençale (Serves 4)

Ingredients

4 cups peeled, diced tomato

1 cup chopped fresh basil

1 T minced garlic

½ cup oil-cured olives, pitted and chopped

Pinch crushed red pepper flakes

2 T capers

¼ cup red wine vinegar

¼ cup extra virgin olive oil

Directions

1. Use your hands to break up the canned tomatoes, leaving them in small chunks. (You could use a food processor, but the machine over-processes them.)

2. Combine all ingredients in bowl and mix well.

3. Heat the sauce in a large skillet and toss with cooked pasta.

Dining in the Age of Global Trade

A S A CHILD GROWING UP, certain holidays were associated with specific foods. My mother loved asparagus, and Mother's Day fortunately falls during the peak of local asparagus season. My father's birthday in the beginning of June was always celebrated with a blueberry pie, in part because that was the beginning of blueberry harvest, at least in the Carolinas if not New England. We treasured these associations in part because, in the early 60's, these ingredients were simply not available any other time of year. It was unimaginable to be able to eat asparagus in January or blueberries in February. Part of the pleasure and enjoyment of eating a blueberry pie in June was that we had endured

months of deprivation, and now we were rewarded with the annual ritual of my father's birthday blueberry pie.

Fifty years later we live in a very different world. While it is still nearly impossible to buy a decent tomato in the winter no matter how much you spend, you can indeed buy asparagus and blueberries in January, even if raised with standard commercial practices. When South American countries like Chile and Peru were first developing these crops for export 20 or so years ago, the quality was not very good, and the price was high. It was easy then to maintain a commitment to eating seasonally and locally, in part because the asparagus spears were tiny, and frequently mushy, in addition to being quite expen-

sive. Likewise the berries were costly, yet small and not very flavorful. Twenty years later, both the quality and price have dramatically improved. In the dead of winter in the Berkshires, it's tempting to buy these ingredients.

If one truly adhered to eating only locally raised farm products, by this time of year we would be mostly dining on root vegetables. Most of us still want to eat fruit and salad year round, and very few people forswear eating chocolate, coffee, oranges and bananas because they're not locally grown. As in the observance of religious practice, we pick and choose what to eat according to what makes sense to us, even if it is somewhat arbitrary and not entirely logical.

While it is not an act of infidelity to our local farmers to buy fruit or vegetables out of season when there is none available locally, it is an act of infidelity to our natural resources and environment. What pesticides and chemicals were used to grow these crops? How much oil did it take to ship them here? How were the workers who toiled in the field paid? These are some of the reasons why locally raised sustainable food costs more. While we may at times succumb to the temptation of the fruits of global trade, it only deepens our appreciation for those seasonal fruits and vegetables, whose time will come. In the meantime, let's eat some root vegetables.

Rutabaga with Hazelnuts

Rutabagas are surely one of the most ignored and under-appreciated vegetables in this country. Their popularity in Scandinavia and the British Isles never quite transferred over to this side of the Atlantic. Originally a cross between a cabbage and turnips, today they are essentially just a variety of turnip, without much resemblance to cabbage. They are clearly in need of a makeover, and some dressing up. Rutabagas have a slightly nutty flavor, which is accentuated by the addition of hazelnuts and hazelnut oil in the following recipe. Though most recipes for root vegetables call for adding butter into the puree, hazelnut oil is a pleasant surprise.

Rutabaga with Hazelnuts

(Serves 4)

Ingredients

2 lb. rutabaga

¼ cup toasted hazelnuts, coarsely chopped

2 T hazelnut oil

Directions

1. Peel and dice the rutabagas.

2. Bring a small pot of salted water to boil. Add the rutabaga and cook for about 15 minutes, until soft, then drain.

3. Puree the cooked rutabaga in a food processor, adding the hazelnut oil as you puree.

4. Serve with a sprinkle of chopped toasted hazelnuts on top.

CASTLE STREET CAFE
GREAT BARRINGTON, MASSACHUSETTS

❧ SPRING ❧ SUMMER 1989 ❧

❧ APPETIZERS ❧

SOUP DU JOUR – $2.50

*GRILLED SHIITAKE MUSHROOMS, GARLIC ❧ HERBS – $4.

*CHILLED ASPARAGUS, SESAME SAUCE – $3.50

SUMMER VEGETABLE TERRINE – $4.

STEAMED MUSSELS, TOMATO ❧ GARLIC – $3.

GRILLED HOMEMADE VEAL SAUSAGE, WHOLE GRAIN MUSTARD – $4.

❧ SALADS ❧

*MIXED GREENS – $2.

WARM SALAD OF ITALIAN CHICORY,
    BACON ❧ CROUTONS – $3.50

*BEET ❧ ENDIVE SALAD,
    WALNUT OIL VINAIGRETTE – $3.

AVOCADO ❧ SHRIMP SALAD – $6.

❧ PASTAS ❧

(HALF ORDERS AVAILABLE AS APPETIZERS)

*LINGUINI PROVENCALE (TOMATO, GARLIC, BLACK OLIVES, CAPERS) – $6.

*FETTUCINI, COLUMBIA COUNTY GOAT CHEESE, TOASTED PECANS – $8.

3 LITTLE PIG PASTA (HOMEMADE SAUSAGE, PROSCUITTO ❧ BACON) – $9.

❧ MAIN COURSES ❧

(SERVED WITH MIXED GREEN SALAD)

GRILLED CORNISH GAME HEN, MARINATED LEMON ❧ HERBS – $10.

COQ AU VIN (CHICKEN BRAISED IN RED WINE) – $11.

ROAST HALF DUCKLING, BLACKSTRAP MOLASSES SAUCE, WILD RICE – $12.50

MEDALLIONS OF VEAL, HUNTER STYLE (VEAL STOCK, MUSHROOMS, TOMATO) – $14.

CALVES LIVER, ONION MARMALADE ❧ GLAZED PEARL ONIONS – $11.

CASTLE BURGER (HALF POUND) – $6.

STEAK AU POIVRE, STRAW POTATOES – $15.

COHO SALMON STUFFED WITH MUSHROOM MOUSSE, CUCUMBER-DILL SAUCE – $13.

SAUTEED SEA SCALLOPS PRIMAVERA – $12.

POACHED FILET OF SOLE, PINK GRAPEFRUIT ❧ ORANGE BUTTER SAUCE – $12.

*EGGPLANT ROULADE, STUFFED WITH 3 CHEESES – $10.

❧ ACCOMPANIMENTS ❧

*ZUCCHINI FRITTERS - $2.50

*SAUTEED BROCCOLI, GARLIC & EXTRA-VIRGIN OLIVE OIL - $2.50

*STRAW POTATOES - $2.50

*WILD RICE - $2.50

*HOMEMADE ONION RINGS - $2.50

*GRILLED PEASANT BREAD, GARLIC & OLIVE OIL - $2.50

❧ DESSERTS ❧

WORLD'S BEST CHOCOLATE MOUSSE CAKE (NEWSDAY) - $2.75

WARM APPLE CRISP, HOMEMADE VANILLA ICE CREAM - $2.75

CREME BRULEE - $2.75

WARM BREAD PUDDING, SOUR MASH WHISKEY SAUCE - $2.75

CASTLE STREET ICE CREAM SUNDAE - $2.75

HOMEMADE ICE CREAM & SORBET - $2.75

FRESH FRUIT - $2.75

FRUIT & CHEESE PLATE - $4.

COFFEE, DECAFFEINATED COFFEE, TEA - $1.   ESPRESSO - $1.50   CAPPUCCINO - $1.75

MICHAEL BALLON, CHEF PROPRIETOR

* VEGETARIAN

OVER, PLEASE

Our first menu — Spring, 1989.

CASTLE STREET CAFE
GREAT BARRINGTON, MASSACHUSETTS

WE THANK AND ACKNOWLEDGE OUR BERKSHIRE NEIGHBORS, FARMERS, PURVEYORS AND FRIENDS FOR PROVIDING US WITH THE FINEST AND FRESHEST LOCAL INGREDIENTS, MAKING IT POSSIBLE TO SERVE DELICIOUS FOOD. WE LOOK FORWARD TO HELPING THIS LIST GROW.

BREADS	DAILY BREAD
	THE BAKER'S WIFE
	GEORGE'S BREAD
MILK	HIGHLAWN FARM
HONEY	CHARLES ZANINI
PRODUCE	TAFT FARMS
	THE CORN CRIB
	WINDY HILL FARM
	BLUEBERRY HILL FARM
CHICKEN & EGGS	OTIS POULTRY FARM
MUSHROOMS	DELFTREE SHIITAKE MUSHROOMS
GOAT CHEESE	LITTLE RAINBOW CHEVRE
	RAWSON BROOK FARM
COHO SALMON	BANCROFT MILL FARM
PASTA	PASTA PRIMA

MAPLE SYRUP   LOWLAND FARM

ESPRESSO   BERKSHIRE COFFEE ROASTING COMPANY

FLOWERS   DOLBY FLORIST

PLEASE, NO SMOKING IN THE DINING ROOM. CIGARETTE SMOKING AT THE BAR.
MAJOR CREDIT CARDS ACCEPTED. MINIMUM CHARGE - $15.
THE CAFE IS AVAILABLE FOR CATERING & PRIVATE PARTIES.

10 CASTLE STREET   GREAT BARRINGTON, MASSACHUSETTS   413-528-5244

The back of our first menu.
Farm to Table since 1989.

PART IV

Profiles in Farming

· ·

Ted Dobson: Equinox Farm

Ted Dobson has been farming in the Berkshires since 1982. After studying agronomy at the University of California at Santa Cruz, Ted returned east. He pulled up to his family land in Hillsdale, NY, driving a 1960 Chevy panel truck, towing a trailer with a donkey in it. Though the farm has been located in three different places, one constant has been that Ted has been the premier grower of organic salad greens for over 30 years.

Ted Dobson: My wife and I crossed the country looking for a place to farm, and I remembered my family's land in Hillsdale, and when we got here, we said. "This is it". We were initially trying to be self-sufficient, and can our own food, but when I got my first tax bill, I realized I needed to make some money, so I hit the pavement trying to sell vegetables.

Michael Ballon: In the beginning, you grew a lot of vegetables, not just salad greens, right?

TD: We grew everything — cauliflower, watermelon, cantaloupe, and a lot of unusual varieties — like purple Afghani carrots, purple broccoli rabe. We sold to the Berkshire Co-op, the Hawthorne Valley Store. Growing these unusual crops is what got me going to Manhattan, because, what was I going to do with all this stuff? Mesclun was a totally new phenomenon, and I distinctly recall selling mesclun in Manhattan in 1986 for $24/lb.! That sure made it worth it to travel there and sell to restaurants.

MB: At least from my point of view, it's a good thing the price has dropped! How many people grow mesclun now around here?

TD: I think everybody is growing their own version of mesclun — but back in the mid 80's, I was the only one. It was a wonderful time to be doing this — because I was in on the ground floor with some of the best chefs in New York and Boston. Those chefs were introducing restaurant goers to new and interesting vegetables, like mesclun, Chioggia beets, braising greens, and baby vegetables, and that created demand in other restaurants. People wanted to know where they could buy these vegetables.

MB: At the time, I was working in Manhattan at *Lavin's*. It was a very high profile restaurant, and we very much felt the influence of the new wave of cooking, as well as the incredible surge of wine from California. It's become ubiquitous now, but at the time I was buying goat cheese from Laura Chenel in California, and having it shipped to New York, because she was one of the very first producers of goat cheese in America. So imagine my surprise and pleasure when one weekend in the Berkshires, in 1982 or so, I discovered Little Rainbow Chevre making goat cheese in Hillsdale New York, just a short way down the road from your farm. I remember thinking, "Wow, they're making goat cheese right here in Hillsdale." So instead of paying a lot of money to ship goat cheese from California, I started supplying my restaurant with Berkshire Chevre. They have since stopped making cheese, but they were making really unusual varieties, including several types of firm, aged goat cheese.

TD: One of the things that happened was that chefs starting using these new greens in different ways, which really changed the whole concept of what salad is.

MB: Yes, that's right. Up until that time salad had been a single leaf, pretty much served by itself, relegated to a small plate as a side course. Suddenly there was salad as part of a featured entrée on a large plate. Instead of old fashioned chicken salad with mayonnaise as a lunch entrée, chicken salad became grilled marinated breast of chicken served over a bed of mesclun greens with a sherry wine vinegar and walnut oil vinaigrette. Instead of serving sea scallops in a cream or butter sauce, we started making salads of warm spinach and shiitake mushrooms with sautéed sea scallops.

I meet with catering clients for weddings and other events, and I still occasionally get someone who tells me they want "regular salad", which I take to mean iceberg, rather mesclun or something similar.

TD: (laughing heartily) Yeah, they don't want any of that "irregular salad"!

One of the things that happened in the late 80's, just about the time you opened Castle Street, was that there was a convergence of the organic movement with the local food movement, and with it a more sophisticated culinary trend and awareness. I had been around the organic vegetable scene for a while, and it was frankly not very imaginative. You'd see co-ops selling cabbage and carrots, and not all that much else. In part because of the proximity of New York, and the increasing awareness in the Berkshires, organic farms became increasingly sophisticated. With an interest in growing some unusual varieties of vegetables, there was a focus on the local market. From my point of view, the begin-nings of the local farm movement are right here in the Berkshires.

MB: Do you remember how we met? It must have been pretty soon after the Café opened, because I didn't know you before we opened. By the end of the summer we knew each other well enough to have a pig roast at your farm.

TD: It must have been just after you opened. You hit the ground running hard, and at some point I just stopped by with some greens. I explained what I did, and you got it immediately, and said, "Hey, start bringing some of this stuff by."

MB: That's right. My opening menu had two sides, and on the back I listed 18 different local purveyors, includ-ing bread, cheese, dairy, and vegetables. I didn't know about you and your farm when I first opened, which is why I didn't list you among the purveyors, but shortly afterwards I was buying a lot of greens from you. And so just a few months later, at the end of the summer, the idea of having a pig roast at your farm was really appealing.

TD: Yes, it was appealing for everyone except my poor son. Ben was about 5 at the time, and I had given him piglet in the spring, without much thought as to how big it would grow, and how difficult it would be to handle. By the end of the summer it was breaking out of the rickety pen we had, and causing havoc in the neighbor's yard.

MB: And so on the Sunday after Labor Day we put a closed sign on the front door of the Café, and invited guests and regular customers to a pig roast with directions and an explanation of what was going on. This was in the days before email and Facebook, so invitations were extended the old fashioned way, literally face-to-face.

TD: I also clearly remember some dinners you invited me to very early on that were designed to introduce different farmers to each other, and to foster some networking among us. So we had some dinners with a dairy farmer you introduced me to, as well as the guy who would become my partner for a while.

MB: I was interested in meeting different farmers, and realized that many of them worked so hard that they didn't know each other. It seemed to me the best way to do this was to sample some of each other's food over dinner.

TD: There were chefs in the 80's here in South County who really were instrumental in creating this farm-to-table movement. It makes me happy to look around and see what's happened in 30 years. It's interesting that chefs like you and Dan Smith from (John Andrews Restaurant) moved to the area at the exact same time, you from New York City, and Dan from Florida, and though your restaurants feel quite different, you each had a similar vision.

MB: One of the things that is nice about the Berkshires is that there is a community of chefs who share similar values, and who recognize that the area is stronger and better for having a concentration of restaurants that are going to be a magnet for visitors to the area. Many of us are buying from some of the same farms, yet the way

we use ingredients is different, and our menus end up reflecting the individual personalities of the chef. We see each other at a variety of charity events that feature food and chefs, and I think there is a real sense of collegiality.

I have one last question before we wrap up. Where do you see farming going in the coming years?

TD: I think the next step is for local farms to start growing commodity crops in a big way. Overwhelmingly, the biggest crop around here is corn, but almost all of it is GMO corn. A lot of people who shop in the Co-op or at Farmers markets already embrace the idea that food should be healthy and local, but we need to take it to the next level, so that we're also growing local and sustainable corn and wheat.

Rawson Brook Farm

By Susan Sellew, Cheesemaker

I WAS PART of the back to the land movement of the 60's and 70's. After attending Antioch College for three years, I opened a small leather shop in Great Barrington where Eagle Shoe is now and received college credit for the endeavor. The taste of self-employment was delicious. With my tools and a stack of suede in various colors, I moved to Boulder, Colorado, where I supported myself making brightly colored leather hot pants. A signature feature of these shorts was the buttons I fashioned from slices of deer antler my dad had found in the woods here in Monterey, where Rawson Brook Farm is today.

One day I walked into The Whole Earth Catalog retail store — and my world shifted. I walked out with my new bible, Rodale's How to Grow Fruits and Vegetables by the Organic Method, and a book published in 1947 called Land for the Family.

We (my then husband Wayne Dunlop and I) moved to Maine, where I bought my first goats in early 1971 a milker and a young kid. Even though my first vivid childhood nightmare involved the neighbor's goat Suki climbing up my bedroom curtains, I was now smitten with these lovely beings. The first afternoon it took the two of us 45 minutes to milk the mischievous jet black Vengetta — we were all such novices. It was a messy affair that yielded no drinkable product — the milk spilled and splattered everywhere. After a week we were proudly filling our one half gallon bucket with absolutely clean milk with about four minutes of effort. I planted my first garden often scooting along on my butt

with the young kid, Eunice, sitting on my lap. I was in heaven.

Towards the end of that year, we moved (with our goats, bees, pigs and freezer full of food) to impoverished northern New York, then a haven for many young land seeking folks like us. With Wayne's brother and wife, we bought, for $18,000 a 260 acre farm with a house, dairy barn, old horse barn, and garage. They took out a loan for the down payment, and we paid the former owner the $102 monthly mortgage payment. Wayne and I had 60 of the acres, the house, and the other buildings. Our life was jam-packed with experiences growing, foraging, and preserving all sorts of things. Along with the lovely and always entertaining goats there were pigs, rabbits, laying hens, turkeys, meat chickens, big gardens, you-pick-it strawberries, maple syrup, honey bees, calves, draft horses, and so on. We learned to graft fruit trees, smoke hams, grow grain, pickle things in crocks, and take our hay in loose, make tortillas with our own dried corn and wood ashes from the kitchen cook stove. One year we spent $200 at the grocery store.

Eventually I attended a cheese making workshop sponsored by the St. Lawrence County Agricultural Extension and presented by Martine Gadbois, a French cheese maker from Montreal. Because I was so infatuated with the goats, my herd had grown to fourteen at that time, and although I made cheese, it wasn't consistently good. Many times it was quite awful. Martine got me on track, and I felt another shift, I absolutely knew what I wanted to do.

It became clear that we would have to move. It was heart wrenching to leave the farm and all our friends, but there would be no local market for goat cheese — the average family income was $400 per year in our town. We considered other locations that would have potential markets before realizing what we really wanted was to come home to the Berkshires. I had grown up in New Marlboro and Wayne in Monterey. If we couldn't sell our cheese in this ideal location, halfway between New York and Boston, we would simply have to do something else. The first challenge of course was the Berkshire economy, especially real estate. It was way out of our league, but things have a way of working out.

In the fall of 1978 we moved. After a false start

in Sandisfield, my dad agreed to give us some of his wooded land in Monterey, seven acres of a larger parcel his grandfather had given him for his twenty-first birthday. Upon returning from Europe after World War Two, he had built a log cabin on the Monterey land, and every summer we would rent our house in civilized New Marlboro, and move three and a half miles over North Road to our log cabin in the woods. I spent much of my childhood wandering in these woods; I love this piece of land like family. Our plan was to clear it and build a farm from scratch.

Looking back, I wonder why my father was willing to let us start this crazy project on his property. What if we lost interest and left a great big mess? No one thought it a wise endeavor; we had framed a letter from the Soil Conservation Service in Pittsfield saying that it was most impractical to think of clearing a wooded piece of land for a dairy farm and they wouldn't advise it. In addition, no one was yet making goat cheese commercially in the United States, although there was talk of Laura Chenel in California. Did my father actually believe in our project, or was it that he just couldn't say no to his daughter?

The first week of January 1979 we started cutting trees on what would eventually become Rawson Brook Farm. By "we" I mean primarily Wayne and myself, and my mother, and our family friend Coleman Nimick, a retired gentleman banker from new Marlboro who wore white flannel pants.

The learning curve was steep. After the first week we barely had a spot opened up big enough for a barn; maybe everyone was right and this was indeed a foolish way to go about things. It wasn't looking good. But by the second week we could keep the fires going through the deep snow, and Wayne could drop a tree exactly where he wanted it to go. We got into a rhythm. My 100-pound 63 year old Italian mother often arrived at the work site before we had even gotten out of bed. She brought home made lunch and other snacks in a big basket, worked with us all day, and then around 4 PM would say, "You two must be exhausted. How about coming over to the house for some dinner? I'll run home and get it ready."

This went on for 83 days; we worked nearly every day until the snow was gone and the fires started getting away from us. Nearly done at that point, we were working our way down the back hill and had exposed a view of the ridge behind Rawson Brook, my father came in to check in after work one day and teared up when he saw the vista out over the swamp and the hillside. We were on a roll. We had delusions of opening things up all the way to New Marlboro.

I have to add that all the while the rumors were circulating around town. They are going to do what? There was talk of the awful clear cutting that was going down on New Marlboro Road. Wayne told one busy body that we were putting in a mini-mall.

Once the cutting and burning was over, we paused and took a good look at ourselves. We had singed eyebrows and lashes, flying cinders had rendered our clothes full of little burned spots, and Coleman could no longer bring his not quite white flannel pants to Reid's cleaners with anything close to a plausible explanation of what had happened to them, so we threw them into the last fire. We now had seven acres of open land strewn with pine saw logs, stacks of firewood, and a sea of stumps.

Wayne set up a small saw mill and milled the pine trees we felled into lumber we used to build the barn. We cut, split, and sold fire wood to pay for some bull-

dozer work. The bulldozer popped the stumps out, all the while reserving the topsoil in piles that were later distributed. We began the days and days of picking roots and stones by hand before seeding a suitable cover crop on the area destined for the future market garden and a permanent pasture mix on the rest.

Along with some market gardening, I did what I called my first test marketing — making cheese in the house and selling it along with the vegetables from a little stand at the end of the driveway. When there were no vegetables to sell, the cheese was sold from our home refrigerator, self-service. I once came home to find three people I had never met sitting on the couch while a fourth was picking out his cheese from the fridge. It was great fun. Another day a customer's child turned on all the burners atop the gas cook stove, and since there was no pilot light, the house filled up with propane. We had to get the barn finished soon!

Before we could legally market our product, the barn had to be totally completed with the milk house and cheese room meeting state and federal standards. There was no one to tell us how to achieve this. There were no places we could go to buy exactly what we needed. We had to exercise all our research and ingenuity skills. In the fall of 1983 we passed our first State Inspection and we were granted a license.

What a haul! I wrote to Martine Gadbois (my French cheese-making mentor from Montreal) and proudly told her the Big News. She wrote back saying she no longer made goat cheese since there was no money in it.

We had a party on the Sunday of Columbus Day weekend to celebrate. Everyone who had helped and supported us came. Folks came who had put up their money so we could get the first Share Loan, a precursor of our local currency, *Berkshares*. We needed this money for windows and our first printing of labels and flyers. Curious people came to see what this goat farm looked like. Those who liked small and humble were delighted; others wondered what all the fuss was about. I cooked up a storm and made a wide selection of goat cheese dishes for sampling. The chocolate goat cheese truffles were the biggest hit.

In the fall of 1983, with the blessing of the various inspection agencies, we were ready to actively (and legally) market Monterey Chevre. I had been making cheese in my kitchen for years and over time had tweaked the various procedures to achieve a product I was happy with. Now the goal was to move to the new cheese room and duplicate the process with entirely different, albeit more appropriate equipment.

The transition into business mode required ongoing education; there was no computer, no internet, and it was hard to find appropriate information. The bookshelves were full of volumes about cheese making, FDA requirements, business bookkeeping, goats and animal health, instructional pamphlets, magazine articles, lists of suppliers of everything from dairy detergent to cheesecloth fabric and prospective contacts and markets that might be interested in our cheese.

We had to shift gears. The goats had only been milked by hand, but now we had the proper set up to be able to use a milking machine. This brought a whole new set of challenges; although quite handy, milking machines can be injurious to the goats' udders if not handled properly and there are many places within them for bacteria to hide. Previously I had been pasteurizing milk on the kitchen stove in a five gallon stainless steel milk can surrounded by hot water in a big pot that was designed for canning vegetables. It took up two burners on the stove top. Now we were doing it in a vat that was actually a pasteurizer. We gradually got familiar with the ins and outs of the new equipment.

When I was designing the buildings for Rawson Brook Farm, I had the firm belief that making cheese from the milk of 25 goats would be an ideal size to aim for. I went even so far as to think it was wise to economize on the amount of available space, not only for financial reasons, but because it would encourage efficiency and actually discourage us from expanding. How I supported this position is vague to me now, but I know I was strongly behind it at the time.

After the first year of operation it became clear that the overhead and expenses to run the business far exceeded our estimations and we were not breaking even. I don't mean that in the standard business sense where the owner's personal salary is included in the calculation. I mean that there was no money left over for us to live on. It seemed that we had two choices: either get bigger and see if that might miraculously turn the tables or hang up our hats with a now-experienced understanding that this economic piece is why you don't see a goat farm on every corner.

Over the next five to six years we steadily added more goats as we simultaneously endeavored to add more capacity to the original building and equipment. Turns out I had only been about 100% off the mark in my initial thinking. As we got closer to 50 milking animals, we could imagine not having other side jobs to keep our heads above water.

For those who like numbers: in 1985 we milked 24 animals and made 7500 pounds of cheese. By 1991 we were milking 50 and made 15,500 pounds of cheese. Last year we made 18,000 pounds of cheese with only 41 milking goats. This trend of "more cheese with fewer goats" in recent years is a reflection of 30 years of practice and fine tuning of animal nutrition and management. The learning curve continues, and keeps me coming back for more.

One might think that as the herd numbers increased, the goats might have lost their individuality, but goats have big personalities. I find that we all still delight in talking and gossiping about them as if they were quirky neighbors. They often have familial traits and personalities that stand out even more because of our naming system, which is based on those familial lines. We have a line of Indian food that began with Chapati. Her offspring have included Naan, Samosa, Panir, Paratha, Tali, Tikka, Lentil, Channa Dahl, Biryani, Patia, Lassi, Dosa, and Chai. One dark and stormy Saturday night, Chai gave birth to a jet black baby girl who was instantly dubbed Chai Noir, with a nod to Garrison Keillor.

Other lines have included names from the world of E.B. White, celestial references, queens, woody shrubs, local women artists, gemstones, palette colors, characters Julia Roberts has portrayed in the movies, sea shells, and small goats whose names begin with "E". Here are some examples of each: Charlotte, Vega, Noor, Lonicera, Edith, Onyx, Alizarin, Darby, Nutmeg, and Etui. We love coming up with names.

We have also added a line of goats named after all the people who have worked at the farm. These folks have given precious time from their lives to Rawson Brook Farm, and I am incredibly grateful to them. I would not be able to indulge in this life of farmer/cheesemaker if it were not for the team effort. They work hard, like to laugh, and most of all, they pride themselves on doing the quality of work that results in excellent cheese. It was my daughter Tarsi who first referred to them as our farm family.

Elizabeth Keen and Al Thorp — Indian Line Farm

Elizabeth Keen and Al Thorp own and operate **Indian Line Farm** in Great Barrington. Indian Line was one of the first Community Supported Agriculture farms in the country when it was started in 1985 by Robyn Van En. Elizabeth and Al rented the land in 1997 and started a small, two-acre market garden, growing for restaurants and farmers' markets. Indian Line Farm is located in South Egremont, Massachusetts, along a strip of land once known as the "Indian Line."

MB: When you first took over Indian Line Farm, would you have imagined that 20 years later there would be thirty-something Community Supported Agriculture Farms (CSAs) in Berkshire County?

EK: No. When Al and I got here, it was under the unfortunate circumstances of someone dying. We essentially started from nothing — there wasn't actually a business here.

MB: You worked with Robyn Van En, the founder of the farm?

EK: I had finished my apprenticeship here at Mahaiwe Harvest, another CSA. Al and I were a new couple, and when we were done with our apprenticeship, we were trying to figure out what to do. Al was planning to go back to Rhode Island, and I was going to return to Washington DC to work for a Latin American think

tank. I got a call from a friend at the Berkshire Regional Land Council, who told me that Robyn was looking for help organizing a conference, and that my organizing skills would be a perfect match. She needed a lot of help organizing the finances of a nonprofit, and I managed to get a 501(c)3 for her. I also just answered the telephone and sent out materials she created. So that was the capacity in which I worked for three months, and then she suddenly died at a tragically young age.

MB: Your organizational skills have always impressed me. I think you were the first farmer I did business with who sent out weekly emails with the list of what was available. You included not just the price, but also what was abundantly available, and what was available on only a limited basis. I find that tremendously helpful. If there is one thing you can count on, it's getting an email from you Sunday night detailing what is available for the following week. We have come a long way from the old days when someone would just show up outside my back door with a box of produce wanting to sell me some.

EK: I do have organizational skills, and I brought them to farming, and that has helped me be successful. But I have also learned from other farmers, and from chefs like you, about what you are interested in, and how and when to make deliveries. When I first started it was before email, so the only way to communicate was to call up someone, or to stop by their business. I remember

when I first met you, and I recall that you were very tough, and were very clear about how you wanted to buy vegetables.

MB: I hope I wasn't too tough!

EK: No, I think you have a tough reputation in terms of what you want, but I think that's ok. The one thing I got from the very first time I met you was that you made it clear you really wanted to buy from local farms.

MB: Indian Line is now a combination of CSA and the market farm, which sells to both farmers' markets and restaurants. That works pretty well for you, right?

EK: There is quite a mix among CSAs — some only sell to shareholders, but certainly many other across the country are a hybrid like us.

MB: If you produce more vegetables than the CSA is going to consume, why not sell it to someone else who wants to buy them?

EK: In fact the main reason why people stop being a member of a CSA is because they are given too much food. You end up filling people's bags with so much kale and green beans and turnips, that they can't deal with it.

MB: Why not lower the share price, so people get a manageable amount of vegetables, and then sell the rest?

EK: That is essentially what I have been doing. I have honed down the share size so that pretty much everybody is happy. I am very aware of what the retail value of a share of vegetables is, and we are very competitive. We often make available additional vegetables for those who want more, but there are very few people who take additional vegetables.

MB: When you factor in the number of times a week people eat out, which for many is a pretty significant number, and if you have this gigantic harvest of vegetables, and you're not cooking at home a lot, it's more food than you can eat.

EK: CSAs attract only a certain kind of person — obviously the kind that tends to cook at home a lot. You might have to forgo a night out to eat your vegetables!

MB: What percent of your business is the CSA, and what is the market garden?

EK: It's almost exactly half and half, with the farmers' markets a very important part of our business, account-ing for about 25-35% of the market sales.

MB: Everybody knows that there is an abundance of vegetables from local farms around here during the summer, but I have to say that it is absolutely mind boggling to walk into the winter farmers' markets and see this incredible display of spinach, turnips, cabbage, bok choy, and see this extraordinary display of vegetables in November and December. You'd think we were in California — but we are in the Berkshires. It's amazing.

EK: It is amazing. I am sometimes flabbergasted myself — it's just those two greenhouses over there (pointing), and they are not even heated. So for the winter markets I am actually harvesting spinach, cilantro, mustard greens, Japanese turnips, radishes, beet greens, chard, and kale.

MB: You expect to see maple syrup, bread, and cheese at winter farmers' market, and maybe some bedraggled vegetables from somebody's root cellar — but the array of vegetables on your table is absolutely pristine.

EK: Some people are committed to not washing the dirt off the vegetables they store in root cellars, but we find that if you don't, the dirt really sticks to the vegetables, and it's not as appealing.

MB: Since Indian Line Farm is the first CSA farm, do you find that you are asked a lot to explain what a CSA is, or that you have a responsibility to do so?

EK: Yes, I get asked a lot. I hadn't even graduated from high school when this farm was organized as the first CSA. There are some very big shoes to fill here. I can honestly say that we have surpassed what was here before we got here.

MB: Yes, I think so. The whole standard and level of farming in Berkshire County has been raised tremendously. Could you have imagined half a dozen cheese makers within a small radius of here? I once said that while there was an abundance of vegetables, there wasn't really much local meat raised here –but that isn't true anymore.

EK: Al and I were this new couple farming, and we didn't know anybody like us when we started 16 years ago, and that's really changed.

MB: You don't have any animals here at all?

EK: No. Early on we had very high hopes to have an integrated farm, and Al and I had both worked on a biodynamic farm. But we quickly realized how little we knew about growing vegetables, and even less about raising animals. Given that we didn't grow up in farming, we didn't have a huge attachment to having a ton of work in the winter time.

MB: Given that you and Al don't come from a farm background, would you like to see your kids take over the farm?

EK: Yes, that would be amazing, but I would like them to come to that decision on their own.

MB: One of the things that is being lost in America today is the kind of knowledge of working on small farms — planting seeds, weeding, milking cows, and harvesting crops that very few people have anymore. A century ago most Americans grew up on small farms, but that is not true anymore.

EK: I love that my kids are growing up on a farm. They learn things about the natural world that their peers don't know.

MB: Do you encounter people at the farmers' market who say, "Where is Indian Line Farm," or who want to visit?

EK: I don't encourage people to visit whenever they want — just like you probably don't want people to stop by your restaurant whenever they want. But if people want to stop by, I am open to it.

MB: Would you say that people who are shareowners get to know each other because of the dynamic of picking up their vegetables?

EK: Yes.

MB: It's sort of like belonging to the same congregation.

EK: Yes. But probably more so because of my weekly emails, in which I get to do some creative writing. People do feel like they belong to something. And I try to foster this through my weekly communication with them.

MB: Do you have volunteers on the farm?

EK: Yes, we have both paid employees and interns who volunteer.

MB: How many shareholders do any work on the farm?

EK: Very few. We used to ask that everyone work 2 hours a season, we have stopped asking that.

MB: I know that others CSAs ask shareholders to do some work on the farm.

EK: Yes, *Caretaker Farm* in Williamstown still asks shareholders to do some work.

MB: It changes the whole way you view the farm and the food you get, if you have to spend some time bending down picking weeds. You're not just a spectator or a customer.

EK: Yes it does. I have been surprised how much difficulty people have showing up to do work.

MB: In America today, I can't imagine a more valuable form of therapy than for people to disconnect from their electronic devices and to spend some time in a beautiful place like Indian Line Farm weeding carrots. I think it ought to be a requirement.

EK: I absolutely love the people who come to work, even if just once a season — and they do have a connection here.

MB: Yes, I would think so.

EK: I have thought if something horrible or apocalyptic happened the whole nature of our farm would change. There would be a lot of people who needed food, and there would be a lot of people willing to work here. That would really change people's connection to the farm.

MB: How have you been effected by the increase in the number of small local farms?

EK: Well, we used to do a lot of business with the Berkshire Co-op Market, but they are making a point of supporting a greater number of farms, and that means they may be buying less from us.

MB: I sometimes feel bad, because during the week I will get half a dozen different emails from various small farmers with their offerings, and I want to support as many as possible. I realize it might seem to you that I am not buying that many vegetables, but I am also buying from quite a few others. Altogether, it's quite a lot. I try to divvy up orders to keep as many farms in business as possible.

EK: Yes, there are more farms to buy from. In the larger scheme of things that is a good thing. It means we all have to continue to be smart and innovate.

MB: Just like you have the experience of many more farms competing for business, look at the explosion in the number of restaurants competing for business. It's the nature of the marketplace, and competition drives us all to be better and smarter. Five years from now there will be more small farmers, and more restaurants.

EK: Yes, it's kind of exciting.

Richard Bourdon — Berkshire Mountain Bakery

Richard Bourdon's Berkshire Mountain Bakery in Housatonic, Massachusetts, was named as one of the Best 10 bread bakeries in America by Bon Appetit Magazine. The bakery is one of the few that mills its own grain daily.

Michael Ballon: You've been doing this even longer than I have.

Richard Bourdon: I started baking in 1978.

MB: I also started Mike's Honest Bread, in 1978. I made about 20 loaves a week, and wrote out the labels by hand. I didn't have a car, and so I a filled a backpack with the bread, and hitch hiked to the local co-op to deliver it.

RB: I started in this country in 1985. I began baking at the Kushi Institute in Becket, Massachusetts. I worked at night, and made everything by hand. I took it to the local Steiner School, and sold it out of the back of my car.

MB: One of the things that seem common to people in the food production business, rather than restaurants, is that when they first start out they made food out of their house, not necessarily with all the required permits or inspection. Now everyone has evolved and grown to have permits and meet all the inspection standards, but in the old days it was possible to begin without that.

I start every day with some Berkshire Mt Bakery bread, with cheese or eggs. Doesn't it amaze you how poor the quality of most bread is in this country?

RB: Yes, the quality of most bread in this country is very poor. Things started going wrong in this country in the 1920's, and 30's, and on from there. And then in the 1980's and 90's there was a resurgence of artisan bakers. I come from the tail end of the hippie generation. I'm not quite a real hippie. We came to a place where we mastered how to make a good loaf of bread. It started out with books like *The Tassajara Bread Book,* making yeasted whole grain bread.

MB: I still have an old copy of The Tassajara Bread Book!

RB: It was just whole wheat flour, water, and yeast and it made bread that was a crumbly mess. And then people started gradually understanding the role of fermentation and sour dough.

MB: Why do you prefer sourdough to yeast? What do you have against yeast?

RB: Yeast on its own would never happen in this world.

MB: But yeast is a naturally occurring thing, in wine, and in other things.

RB: Yes, it's a naturally occurring thing, but if you leave it on its own, the bacteria will always take over. Yeast will always be kept at bay by bacteria. So yeast would never develop the concentration it does in commercial bread, where they select it and grow it separately, and bypass a whole natural process that would otherwise take place. I prefer sourdough over yeast because yeast does not offer acidification. It doesn't acidify the dough. I use sourdough because, if you want to mine or extract nutrients out of grain, you need to let it sour.

MB: And why is that better for people?

RB: The acidity is important because the whole point of the acid is to break down some anti-nutrients in wheat. Our conversation should begin by saying that life feeds on life, but no life wants to be eaten. It's a little bit of a dilemma.

MB: (Laughing) Fortunately, we are on the top of the food chain, so we're mostly doing the eating, rather than being eaten.

RB: We have managed to offset things like viruses, which can take over, and we're always on the lookout. One life knows how to undo the other life. That's a natural process. The last thing wheat has in its mind is to be macaroni on your plate. It never thought that's how it would end.

MB: What did wheat imagine it was going to be?

RB: Wheat imagined it was going to be another wheat plant. And it imagined it would grow tall to catch a lot of sun. Wheat seeds come all packaged in an amazing way — it's a little bit like the batmobile. When it's all locked up it's all protected, and if you try to break into it, you can't. When you hit the little clicker, like in the movie, it opens up. Wheat is the same idea. In that little wheat berry there is everything that is needed for creating new life, all wrapped up tight, and in the right conditions it won't spoil for thousands of years. There are two things in this seed that are important — the first are enzyme inhibitors. This is a substance that prevents the seed from sprouting until conditions are right. The other substance in grain is phytic acid. It's an acid that binds minerals. Soaking or fermenting or sprouting grains allows enzymes, lactobacilli and other helpful organisms to break down and neutralize phytic acid. A diet high in unfermented whole grains, particularly high-gluten grains like wheat, puts an enormous strain on the whole digestive system. Phytic acid is used in rust proofing materials and Rustoleum paint, because it binds to minerals and prevents oxidizing. In order to survive, plant seeds need to prevent themselves from oxidizing until they are planted and start to sprout. Then the minerals start to dissolve, and a new plant starts to form. If you don't do something to break that seed down, to break those anti-nutrients, then they are going to hurt you. We need to break those anti-nutrients down, and that's where the sourdough comes in. The sourdough is making use of the bacterial culture and lactic acid, and one acid dissolves the other acid. The bacteria itself is also out for food. We're all looking for food. In those simple cells, the bacteria have the enzymes and mechanism to hack away at the grain. They break down the minerals, so that they can have them. But little do they know that I am the one who allowed them to live in this particular pool of flour and water, and that now I am going to eat them. I let them do the work, and then I eat them. It's such a sad world. Some people say you are what you eat. I like to say that what you eat becomes you. As long as you do something valuable with what you eat, you are on the right path.

MB: There is increasing interest in eating locally grown food. Do you think it's feasible to raise wheat in the Berkshires for your bread?

RB: No, I don't. It's too wet here. The reason they grow wheat in the Midwest is that it is more arid there, and grain grows best in an arid environment.

MB: Would you say that you are using less white flour than when you started twenty five or thirty years ago?

RB: No. Twenty five years ago I was using all whole grain flour. I came to this country in 1985, and started selling to Bread & Circus, which became Whole Foods, and I was selling nothing but fresh-milled whole grain bread. Then in about 1989 the artisan bread movement started. Everybody was going nuts making artisan bread. The uglier it was, the better it was. I even got comments from people that my bread must be machine made, because it looked too good. That's crazy because humans have much more skill than any machine. I almost got to the point that I said to my guys, 'make the bread ugly, because it sells better.' And then everything shifted back to white flour. Everybody started wanting ciabatta, and I needed to make a living, so I made it. You can eat white flour, and you can eat refined food, but you will have to work hard to restore your balance. I never tell anyone to eat a lot of bread. I always tell people to put butter on the bread. If you take a piece of grain that has been processed properly, milled properly, fermented properly, and cooked properly, and put some raw butter on top that has enzymes in it, and chew it well, like your mamma told you to, it's a healthier way to eat, because the fat slows down the absorption of sugar.

MB: What's your take on the whole gluten-free phenomenon?

RB: That requires a long answer. There are two issues. It

is a digestive issue — some people have trouble digesting gluten. In order to make something easy to eat, it makes sense to try and make it easier to digest. You can't just eat the whole TV. You at least have to grind it down to a powder. Then you could eat it, if you ate a little bit over a year's time, and if you grind it fine enough. But you have to process so it becomes edible.

MB: So aside from the digestive issue, do you think the issue with gluten is that it is being used with yeast?

RB: Yes, that is part of it, but that is not all of it. People think that making bread is something humankind just figured out and discovered. That's not how it happened. Souring grain to make bread is just instinctive. Across the board, throughout the world, indigenous people all sour their grains before they eat them. Now where did they learn this? They did not learn it. It is instinctive. In West Africa they make kenkey, and in Ethiopia they make injera. The grains are always fermented. They ferment the grain using souring, before cooking it, or they cook the grain, and ferment after. The reason for souring is to break down the phytic acid.

MB: So does Berkshire Mountain Bakery bread being made today contain some original starter from ages ago when you first started?

RB: No. Sourdough starter is always there. I could make a new starter any day of the week.

Climbing Tree Farm – Schuyler and Colby Gail

Schuyler and Colby Gail operate Climbing Tree Farm, a small, family farm in New Lebanon, NY. They raise heritage pork, poultry, and lamb, all on pasture and woodland. They are about two decades younger than the farmers previously profiled, and represent the next generation of farmers.

Michael Ballon: Tell me how someone who became a strict vegetarian as an eight year-old girl winds up in the livestock business?

Schuyler Gail: As a kid it was pretty simple. I liked animals and it made me sad that animals were killed to make food. As I learned more I was horrified by the animal cruelty practiced by the commercial meat industry, as well as the environmental and health ramifications of the industry. I was a vegetarian for over two decades and it wasn't until I had been raising animals for slaughter for a few years that I started eating meat. As a vegetarian I ate a lot of beans and cheese, and at some point I realized that the beans I was eating were largely grown in China and the dairy I was consuming directly supported the conventional veal industry. I found my vegetarian diet was neither cruelty free nor environmentally friendly. We grew soy and dried beans for a while, but it isn't easy to produce enough to support a vegetarian diet year-round here. It made sense to eat more locally, and although the idea of eating meat made me squirm, it seemed like a responsible choice to begin raising our own animals for slaughter.

MB: How did you get started farming?

SG: My husband and I were expecting our first child and disagreed about whether our children would be raised vegetarian; our compromise was to raise our own meat. We got our first sheep seven years ago when we were caretakers for the farm where my grandmother grew up. Our son was six weeks old then. We wanted to have meat available for him to eat when he started eating solids, and we needed to find a way to get rid of the tall grass around the barns. Someone gave us eight sheep. We fenced off the barnyard and let the sheep have that part of the farm. They hadn't been sheared for three years and they were so shaggy we couldn't even tell which ones were male or female. We'd never had sheep before.

MB: That makes two of us.

SG: We had them sheared soon after they arrived and discovered we had three rams. We kept one ram and processed the other two. One of the first rams was named Unicorn, because he had only one horn. We still have his skin, we were really proud of it at the time. The ram we kept was named Susie — he was named before the first shearing. The sheep started having lambs, and we started selling the meat to friends and acquaintances.

After we had sheep for a while and found taking care of them meant that we couldn't leave home as easily, we got chickens. The first year we had 25 chickens, the next

year we had 100, and the year after that we had 1,300. I wouldn't recommend that many chickens; we won't do that again.

We never intended to become full-time farmers, but one thing led to another and now it's our job.

MB: Tell me about your farm?

SG: Our goal is to keep our animals true to their instincts: letting our pigs root, our chickens, geese and turkeys range, our sheep graze. Our pigs forage year round on field and forest. We graze rotationally, which rejuvenates our land, rather than degrading it, providing our pigs, which are naturally curious, new things to explore and the highest quality forage possible. We have trained our pigs to "self-load" into their trailer, which helps eliminate stress on slaughter day. We work with two local USDA processors, both of whom are Animal Welfare Approved, and are committed to slaughtering using the most humane methods possible.

MB: Although you began by working your family's farm, you now have relocated to your own place.

SG: Yes. We began experimenting as farmers on the land my grandmother grew up on. It was meaningful to me to learn about farming on the land my great-grandfather once farmed, and not many children can say they were born on their great-great-grandparents farm, like our kids were. We moved off the family farm in its 100th year. It was bittersweet, leaving that family farm and starting our own; like growing up, I guess.

Two years ago my husband and I purchased 20 acres through the Columbia Land Conservancy—a piece of land that had not been farmed for more than 50 years. We bought it from a family who had owned it as a second home. When we moved here it had been brush-hogged irregularly over the past 50 years or so but was mostly goldenrod taller than me and a lot of brambles. Everyone who came to visit asked when we were going to have it mowed, but we didn't. We grazed the pigs, sheep and poultry for a year, and now the fields are fairly decent pasture again. There is some bramble and goldenrod left, but there is also a lot of clover and other desirable plants returning—without having to seed them. Animals can be taught to eat weeds, which still have food value, but are less delicious. In the woods our pigs are clearing out the underbrush and brambles, and we have pasture grasses and clover moving in where the pigs have been.

We are incredibly lucky, because our own land is beautiful, and we were able to sign a lease for a few hundred acres with a neighbor. Land lease is a fantastic arrangement for both the landowner and the farmer. The landowner benefits through tax reduction and the farmer, well, we have more room to grow food and a business. Having plenty of land to use means that we can give the land a healthy rest period, while the animals move on to forage in the next spot. The animals are always moving. Most pig farms are pretty smelly — ours isn't.

MB: So, you let the animals do all the work of clearing the land?

SG: Yes, that's right. We are able to manage our farm with no machinery (other than a very, very beat up pick-up truck) by managing the animals well. I wouldn't say it's any less work, but you rack up fewer monthly equipment payments! We work hard to cut costs, without sacrificing the quality of the product or the comfort of the animals. We have no tractor or barn, and when we say our animals are pasture-raised, we really mean that. We don't have a barn to coop them up in. Farm animals prefer to be outside.

MB: Tell me how you feed the animals. I understand that you help recycle some local food products?

SG: There's a saying that "you are what you eat eats," and we believe it. We work with dairies, and cheese makers, fruit and vegetable farms, breweries, and a local grain mill, to feed our pigs a healthy, varied diet, which gives their meat its distinctive creamy flavor, and fine marbling. About half of our pigs' diet comes from eating the plants growing here on the land. We also get about 300 gallons of whey every week from a local cheese maker. The animals' diets change all of the time, but we're committed to reducing the amount of grain we feed them. It works well for everyone — giving the food away to us is cheaper (and less wasteful) than paying to throw

it out — and we are getting really high quality food for our pigs. In the fall we feed fallen apples, and leftover pumpkins. We planted a pig garden with old-fashioned varieties of hog forages, and the pigs till and fertilize the garden for us, and trample in the seed. Pigs are omnivores. They will eagerly eat anything you set before them. For generations people have routinely fed pigs things they really shouldn't eat — recently that means things as ridiculous as pallets of expired chewing gum,

for example. We feed our animals real food — in fact, my husband Colby sometimes snacks on their grain, and had tried most of the plants in the field.

MB: And do you notice a difference in the flavor of the meat depending on what the animals eat?

SG: I'm a farmer. I can tell you when an animal is healthy, content, and well cared for, and that I'm a pretty big fan of the meat we raise. We rely on chefs, like you, and butchers that we've met along the way to help us improve the quality of our products. At the farmer's market we often sell people their first dozen "farm" eggs or their first pastured chicken. It's fun to see them the next week at the market and ask them how it went. They're always excited to tell us how different, and more flavorful, what we raise is.

In terms of the flavor of our pork — our pigs are healthy, and live the way that pigs are meant to, foraging for food freely in the woods. We are loosely combining pork-raising methods from around the world — Italian pigs are fed dairy left over from the cheese industry, and the resulting pork is great. The flavor of Iberian ham (which is widely regarded as the most delicious in the world) is heavily tied to the acorns the Iberian hogs eat.

Farming is hard work. We don't want to raise a so-so product, so we model our farm after the best. We rotate our pigs so both the fields and the animals maintain the best health.

We feed our pigs according to the season. The pigs that finish in the fall produce a nutty, fruity flavored pork, because they eat a lot of apples and nuts. The pigs that finish in the spring produce a "springier" (for lack of a better word) flavored pork, because they eat more spring grasses, and leafy forage.

The conventional hog farmer strives for rapid weight gain, feed efficiency, low fat content, and uniform pigs. We don't. We raise heritage pigs. Each breed has specific characteristics, as well as each individual pig. Industrial pork producers keep pigs confined in small areas, literally up to their knees in waste. It is no wonder they get sick and need antibiotics

MB: Where do you sell what you raise?

SG: The majority of our pork is sold at restaurants, and butcher shops. We go to the farmers' market weekly for most of the year, and we run a cooperative CSA in our community. Most of our poultry goes to the CSA. It's important to us that real people eat what we grow. We got into this so that our kids could eat good meat, and we want other people's kids to get the good stuff too. There is no reason normal people shouldn't eat the same meat that's served at fine restaurants. And, at the same time we love seeing the meat we raise go to fine restaurants, where it gets royal treatment.

MB: So, what is it like to be a small farmer?

SG: We got our start on my great grandfather's farm, and that is a place that has been important to several generations of my family. This is *my* family's farm, and I want a place where my little boy and baby girl could experience the wonders of life on a farm daily. Fluffy chicks, goslings, turkey poults, lambs, piglets — these kids are lovers of all things cute and baby. They have trees to climb, dirt to dig in (and sometimes eat), and parents who are usually home (though usually working). These kids are faring well. Our farm got its name from the tree our kids like to play on.

MB: You have chosen a life and lifestyle that is quite different from the mainstream ones lived in America today.

SG: A lot of people think our life is very quaint and simple. Some of the people I know from high school tell me that I'm living their dream—having kids and farming. The dream and the reality are probably very different. I had a romantic image of farming, to some degree, when we began farming. I didn't think about the details, like how do you take care of a two year old while you're castrating piglets?

Often, when people hear we are farmers they say something like "oh, how nice, so you have the winters off?" I can't speak for vegetable farmers, because I am not one, but work does not cease on a livestock farm during the winter or otherwise; not in the winter, or on our birthdays, or on Christmas, or when we have the flu. Animals eat, and have needs every day, year round. What does change are the kinds of work we do, the population on the farm, and the weather.

We gain nearly two full days each week after holiday farmer's markets dwindle in mid-late December...which is good and bad. We love seeing our customers each week and depend on the income we make there, but it feels fabulous to eat pancakes and play with play dough on a Sunday morning with our kids.

MB: In many ways your farm restores time honored traditional agricultural practices, which got abandoned in the modern industrial age.

SG: Farming is very much going two opposite directions — uber mechanized and scientific vs. back to the old ways. In many ways the way we are farming pre-dates the way our great, great grandparents (or further back) might have farmed, and at the same time these techniques (like rotational grazing without a fulltime shepherd) are only possible because of technological advancements (like solar powered electric fencing). It's a funny balance.

Most of the things we are learning today were known for centuries, and then got lost. For example, in our grandparents' generation, hogs were kept confined in little, smelly barnyard pens, but if you look farther back, pre-18th century, they roamed relatively freely and relied heavily on forage.

In many ways, our lack of formal farming education has allowed us to break conventions that we never knew to follow, and to make positive changes unknowingly. These things are the things we know for sure: that in farming it's important to do work, and make plans, that keep our family, our animals, our customers, and this specific piece of the earth that we call our farm and our home, safe, healthy, and content.

PART IV

Running a Restaurant

· ·

Being in the Theatre District

IT WOULD BE HARD TO OVERESTIMATE the impact that being next to the Mahaiwe Theatre has had on the Café. Although not large, we are very much located downtown in the Theatre District. Initially the district consisted of only the Mahaiwe and Castle Street Café, but the building of the Triplex Cinema around the corner certainly expanded that by at least a block or two. Most restaurateurs would give their eye teeth to be next to a theatre or performing arts center. The symbiosis between a restaurant and theatre is clear, and at its best, extraordinary. There is an excitement and anticipation each night as the sun sets and the evening begins. We share the daily cadence of preparing during the day, and performance at night. Though we are two separate and independent businesses, we have effectively formed a partnership, and the sum of the parts is far greater than the two alone.

Founding member of the *Berkshire Playwrights Lab* Jim Frangione expressed it well: "My group, The Berkshire Playwrights Lab, started presenting developmental readings of new plays at the Mahaiwe Theater over 6 years ago. In that time I can't remember not going next door to Castle Street after one of our events, to talk with other artists and audience members, to share a glass of wine or two, perhaps over some wonderful dish. These after-show gatherings have become a sort of cultural meetinghouse for us all. In any community, there is a center, a marketplace where ideas flourish and people are engaged in the issues of the day, issues that impact us all. That's what Castle Street Café means to me."

Fortunately for us, those who support the arts also like to go out dinner at a place like Castle Street, before or after the show. It's part of the evening's ritual: dinner and a show. We are grateful to be next to a theatre that attracts so many patrons who also like the restaurant. Regardless of whether it is modern dance, opera, theatre, or popular music, we know that if there is an 8 PM curtain, we will be busy before the show.

In the early years, the Mahaiwe was primarily a movie theatre, and we quickly learned to track the start and ending times of movies, and to keep track of the schedule. Today the Mahaiwe is a performing arts center, and on those nights when The Paul Taylor Dance Company or David Sedaris or the Cowboy Junkies perform, the joint will be jumping. The excitement of going out to a show spills over into the dining room, and raises everyone's energy level. It is far more stimulating to eat in a noisy crowded restaurant than an empty one.

The tough part is convincing diners to allow us enough time to cook their meal to order, and themselves enough time to dine in a relaxed manner. On a busy night when there is no show, guests stagger into the Café gradually over time, and most people are here for a leisurely evening. On the night of a performance, however, it is just the opposite. There is a sudden onslaught of people coming to dinner, and all are trying to get out in time for the show. When questioned why we ask them to come as early for dinner as we do, I remind guests that they are not dining alone, but actually having dinner with 150 other people who are also going to the same show.

One highlight we will never forget is the night when Emanuel Ax was the guest artist at the Mahaiwe. The theater doesn't have a green room with a piano to warm

up on, and we were asked if it would be OK if he warmed up on our piano. Of course we said yes. So, as the Café was jam packed with customers with tickets to the concert, Manny nonchalantly walked into the bar, removed the cover from our piano, and started gracing the room with a Mozart piano sonata. Diners quickly realized that it wasn't the usual music at Castle Street, and when they looked up from their meal, they immediately recognized the virtuoso pianist who they had tickets to see. He did his best to ask people to pay him no attention and continue with their meal. When he finished, he received a rousing ovation, and diners were thrilled to have gotten a little musical hors d'oeuvre before the concert.

On nights when the theatre has popular music, concertgoers can extend their evening out, walk out the door of the Mahaiwe and right in to more music at Castle Street. Since the theatre doesn't have a bar, that is an extra incentive to come next door.

In addition to feeding the concertgoers, we often feed the artists as well. Though they are still jokingly referred to as starving artists, their contracts provide that they be served a meal of their choice, and we often have the task of feeding musicians, dancers, and actors. This is a responsibility that I take seriously, because I figure that an artist is much more likely to perform well after a delicious meal than after a lousy one. It's gratifying to have gotten emails from performers on tour, thanking us for a great meal, and lamenting that the subsequent meals they were served back stage didn't compare.

It's all part of being in the Theatre District.

No One Likes Kohlrabi

No ONE LIKES KOHLRABI, or at least very few people do. How many of us have any idea of what it looks like, or have ever touched, cooked, or eaten one? Not all vegetables are created equal. We are almost all madly in love with fresh corn at the height of the season and local heirloom tomatoes. We thrill at farmer's markets that abound with dozens of different lettuce varieties. In the spring our hearts are lifted by the arrival of local asparagus, which gives us the strength to get through mud season. But how many delight in kohlrabi, or parsnips?

One of the most popular dishes in summer is a plate of sliced local heirloom tomatoes, with the obligatory shredded basil, and fresh mozzarella. It can be served with just red tomatoes, but what really makes the dish is an array of green, yellow, and orange tomatoes. There isn't any cooking involved; it is simply a question of selecting the best and ripest locally grown tomatoes. It's on the Café menu every summer, at least when there isn't a tomato blight, and is consistently very popular.

Our local farmers really shine in this area, and it is practically a requirement of summer. But would you order a cucumber sampler? Well, not many people did when we featured it as a special. The idea is the same, a chance to taste several different and interesting varieties of locally grown, organic heirloom cucumbers. *Farm Girl Farm* grows heirloom cucumbers in amazingly different sizes, shapes and colors. They range from almost white to pale yellow, to pale green and dark green, and have great names like *Boothby's Blondes* and *Super Zagross*. As a chef, the notion of sampling different varieties of the same food is intriguing, whether it's wine grapes, tomatoes, or cucumbers. However, a plate of heirloom cucumbers has not been a popular dish.

And if that's true of cucumbers, what then of the poor kohlrabi? Grated raw and eaten in or mixed with a slaw, kohlrabi has a taste akin to cabbage with a little horseradish root. You have to search long and far to find kohlrabi in a supermarket, let alone on a restaurant menu. If you do encounter it on a restaurant menu, an ambitious chef searching for an ingredient that might shock diners into attention is probably using it. Featured in some outrageous fashion, it is designed to be provocative and attention getting. Yes, kohlrabi crème brulee is something you've never seen or tried before, and it is truly an original idea, but there is a good reason for that.

A restaurant or farm has finite resources, and neither can devote too much time, space or energy to selling or serving what the eating public isn't interested in. People vote with their wallets and we simply like some vegetables more than others. If you don't believe me, go ask the rutabagas and the lima beans.

Basil Puree

A puree of basil is more versatile than pesto. It is simply a puree of basil and olive oil without the nuts, garlic, and cheese in pesto, which makes it much less expensive to make. It can be used to flavor mayonnaise, or in sautéed seafood preparations, in which you might not want cheese or nuts. Stored in the refrigerator, it will last for months. Once you have the food processor out, it is really easy to make a big batch. You will be glad you did. A spoonful of basil puree tossed in some pasta brings back the taste of summer after it is long gone.

If a Tree Falls in the Forest

ONE OF THE OLDEST philosophical conundrums is the question, "If a tree falls in the forest, and no one is there to hear it, does it make any noise?" I have jokingly asked my farmer friends a variation on that question: "If a tomato ripens after Labor Day, and no one is there to eat it, does it matter?" That question is asked out of my frustration that the bounty of the gardens often come too late. It seems that on the first warm day of spring people are clamoring for basil and heirloom tomatoes, even though they are months away.

As the Berkshires gear up for the summer on Memorial Day weekend, the excitement and anticipation is in the air. Yet there really isn't much local produce around, unless you count radishes, which I don't. I have beseeched my farmer friends to go out into the fields and give those tomatoes a good pep talk, so we might have them sooner.

The corollary of this happens in the fall when tomatoes and melons that have been slow to ripen are just coming into their own. Often at their peak in the early weeks of September, the crowds of visitors have significantly diminished by then. Farmers from whom I have been buying large quantities of vegetables all summer long call or email offering me their harvest, and I have to explain that it's a quieter time of year, and I don't need as much. The tomatoes may be the best of the season, but there are fewer people here to eat them.

There are a couple of ways to extend the season. Generally by the end of the season basil is starting to seed, and farmers are harvesting the last of the plants for the year. This is the time to buy a large quantity of basil and puree it for either pesto, or to just puree in oil. Pureed basil lasts for months in the fridge, and retains a lot of flavor. When the ground is covered in snow, there is nothing like throwing some of your own pesto on some pasta to bask in the glow of summer.

Canning tomatoes is a labor-intensive effort, but tomatoes can be slow roasted and dried in an oven to help preserve them. Drying tomatoes in an oven very slowly over many hours evaporates much of the water, which both preserves them and concentrates their flavor. A convection oven is ideal for this, because the circulating air helps dry out the tomatoes. The result is not nearly as dry as commercial sundried tomatoes, but you do get a rich tasting tomato that has more pulp and less liquid. The addition of olive oil and herbs adds a lot of flavor. It is best to cook them in the oven overnight as they require about 8 hours at a very low temperature, and won't warm your house during the already hot day. Once dried, these tomatoes will last another few weeks in the refrigerator, but they don't last forever like canned ones. They can be enjoyed as is, in salads or sandwiches, or pureed.

These are some of the ways to extend the late season harvest, so that when a tomato falls in the garden, someone is there to eat it.

Oven Roasted Tomatoes

(Serves 4)

Ingredients

12 ripe tomatoes
½ t whole peppercorns
A few sprigs fresh thyme
2 cloves garlic, sliced into thin slivers
1½ cups olive oil

Directions

1. Remove the core of the tomato and cut in half. Scoop out the seeds, and place cut side down in a glass or stainless steel baking pan.

2. Pour the olive oil into the pan, and add the peppercorns, thyme, and garlic slivers.

3. Turn your oven as low as it can be set, ideally to 150° or 175°. Bake the tomatoes for about 8 hours.

4. Pour off the olive oil and reserve for later use in dressing. The tomatoes can be eaten immediately when removed from the oven or stored for a week or two in the olive oil in your refrigerator.

A Living Wage

IT HAS TAKEN FAR MORE TIME than it should have, but those concerned about eating healthy food and animal welfare have finally begun to express similar concern about the working conditions of the human beings who prepare their food. While animal rights activists have been successful in pressuring McDonalds to increase the size of their chicken cages, labor activists have not managed to get the company to increase their employee's wages. But that might be starting to change.

In response to some one day strikes at fast food restaurants across the country, President Obama announced a proposal to increase the federal minimum wage from the present $7.25/hour, to $10.00/hour. The current minimum wage is the equivalent of a yearly salary of $15,000, which meets the official U.S. definition of poverty. As the president noted, the real U.S. minimum wage is less than it was when Harry Truman was in office.

Reflecting the legacy of the Saint whose name he chose, Pope Francis has spoken eloquently about the deepening economic divide, and the injustice associated with

such great disparity of incomes. In his first Apostolic Exhortation, Francis dismissed the whole theory of trickle-down economics as unsupported by fact. The Pontiff asked, "How can it be that it is not a news item when an elderly homeless person dies of exposure, but it is news when the stock market loses two points?"

The working poor are heavily concentrated in the fast food industry, which is why there has been such a concentration of strikes and labor actions there. McDonald's CEO earns $9,200 an hour, while the company's average line employee makes $7.73 an hour, according to a recent study by personal finance company NerdWallet.com.

Like almost everywhere in this country, the Berkshires have a smattering of fast food restaurants, but its reputation and character are defined by the unusually large number of independent and chef-owned restaurants. Great Barrington must be one of the very few towns in the country where a Burger King closed, only to reopen as a sushi restaurant. Tipped staff working at virtually any of the upscale inns, resorts, and restaurants in the area are almost certainly earning well above the minimum wage. Because of the historically low unemployment rate in the Berkshires, many employers, including me, have offered starting wages significantly more than the minimum. You get what you pay for.

Author and food activist Michael Pollan has argued, "Instead of paying workers well enough so that they can afford good, honestly priced products — as Henry Ford endeavored to do so that his workers might afford to buy his cars — we pay them so little that the only food they can afford is junk food destructive of their health and the environment's."

I have often fantasized about a form of therapy for those who oppose pay raises for the working poor, including the editorial page of Forbes Magazine. I'd be curious to see how their point of view might evolve after taking out the garbage, mopping floors, and washing dishes in a steamy, busy kitchen for a few months. Those who work in the comfort of air conditioned offices and who transit through the drive-thru of fast food restaurants in new model cars might well find it a revelation if they had to perform some of the labor involved in preparing their own food.

Pasta has always been one of the most affordable meals, and the following recipe should be within the budgets of most of the working poor.

Penne with Arugula, Portabello & Shaved Parmesan (Serves 4-5)

Ingredients

1 lb. penne pasta

3 portabello mushrooms caps, grilled and diced

2 T olive oil

¼ cup diced red onion

2 cloves garlic, minced

3 cups lightly packed fresh arugula

3 T coarsely grated parmesan

Salt & pepper to taste

Directions

1. Cook the pasta, drain, cool, and set aside.

2. Pour the olive oil in a skillet, lightly sauté the onions, then add the mushrooms and garlic.

3. Add the arugula and toss well. Be careful not too overcook the greens, or they will completely wilt. The idea is to only lightly cook them.

4. Add the pasta to the pan, add the cheese and thoroughly mix the greens and mushrooms with the pasta.

5. Taste for salt and pepper, serve hot.

Honoring Service

RECENTLY the three largest hotels and resorts in the Berkshires, and one of the nation's premier liberal arts colleges, as well as TV celebrity Chef Mario Batali, have agreed to multi-million dollar settlements to end lawsuits by employees who claimed that the owners illegally withheld tips. The Berkshire hotels are among the largest employers in the hospitality industry in the area, and Chef Batali employs over 1,000 tipped staff in his many restaurants.

What is it that leads these companies to think that tipped service workers are undeserving of the gratuities they receive?

Fish Tacos (Serves 4)

Ingredients

16 corn tortillas

2 cups finely shredded cabbage

1 cup rice wine vinegar

Juice of 1 lemon

Juice and zest of 1 lime

Four 6-8 oz. pieces of cod, hake, or tilapia

2 tomatoes, diced

2 dry chipotle chilies

2 cups mayonnaise

½ cup coarsely chopped cilantro

Directions

1. Marinate the finely shredded cabbage in the vinegar, lime and lemon juice. Let sit for one hour.

2. Reconstitute the dry chipotle chili by soaking in boiling water for 30 minutes. Drain well, and puree in a food processor with the mayonnaise.

3. Preheat oven to 350°

4. Lightly flour the fish and brown on both sides in a skillet. Place the skillet in the oven for 5 minutes to finish cooking the fish.

5. Drizzle a little oil on the tortillas, and heat in the oven until warm.

6. When the tortillas are warm, place two on top of each other, so there are 8 double thickness tortillas.

7. Divide the fish among the tortillas. Top with the shredded cabbage, diced tomato, and cilantro. Pour some chipotle sauce on top, and serve hot.

Tipped employees are often caught in the middle between difficult and demanding customers, and temperamental, pot throwing chefs, having to navigate successfully between both in order to keep each happy. Many tipped workers only work part time and try to juggle families, careers in the arts, or another full time job. Except for the biggest urban hotels, very few are union members, and part time workers rarely have health insurance coverage from their employer.

The National Restaurant Association reports that almost half of all Americans got their first job in a restaurant, and the vast majority of those were tipped or service jobs. Those who have memories of having once worked for tips are among those most likely to tip well, having endured the trials of being a waiter.

It is an old truism that many restaurants with mediocre food do well, but those with poor service don't last long. The essence of hospitality is making guests feel comfortable and at home, and disgruntled employees tend not to provide good service.

Every restaurant I have ever worked in has provided a staff meal for employees, often referred to as the Family Meal. Many a struggling artist or impoverished dishwasher has been sustained by this Family Meal. It is one of the perks of being a restaurant employee, and though I could choose to eat anything, I make a point of eating the same meal the rest of the staff does. In many ways a restaurant is family, and you don't steal tips from family.

Fish Tacos are a favorite with the staff, popular with those born on both sides of the border.

Listening Local

IN THE CURRENT WORLD OF FOOD, nothing is as holy as local. Everywhere around here there is Farm to Table, farmer's markets, Community Supported Agriculture, and restaurants that feature local provisions. Many area menus, including my own, proudly feature offerings that cover the spectrum from bread and cheese, locally raised grass fed beef and local vegetables in season. We do this in the belief that local is fresher and more sus-

tainable, and because we have relationships and know and trust local farmers. Anyone who had the privilege of being at the Holiday Farmer's Markets this past season in Great Barrington got to see the extraordinary array of locally grown produce still being offered at what would normally be regarded as the end of the season. There was an amazing display of bok choy, broccoli and spinach, as well as many colored root vegetables.

So, if local is good when it comes to food, why isn't local music similarly as well regarded? Locally grown food is considered to be of the highest quality, while far too often, local musicians are referred to as being "local" in a disparaging way. It's almost as if they are only good

enough to play around here, and not beyond. Saxophone great Roland Kirk can be heard on a live recording telling a crowd his band usually played at the same local club most of the time, but that they went out "On The Road." This was every once in a while just to make people think that they had been away, and were therefore somehow more important, and not just a "local band."

The phrase "starving musician" is a part of the lexicon for good reason. Almost none of these people make a living performing, and since there is no cover charge, musicians do not make a big paycheck playing at Castle Street. Most do it for the sheer love of the music. There is a dynamic and thrill to live performance that is unique.

Thirteen years ago when I first had the idea of offering live jazz in Great Barrington, I wasn't at all sure that there was enough local talent to support it. Years later, I know how deep the musical treasure is in the Berkshires and surrounding areas. To snidely refer to them as "just local" musicians is an injustice, and you need only hear them for yourself.

The dearth of jazz clubs in New York City means that even well regarded jazz musicians there can't get a date in their own city. They are therefore willing to travel to Great Barrington, where they can get an opportunity to perform. It should come as no surprise that given the area's deep ties to music that there are some extremely talented people who chose to reside here. Musicians who regularly play here have performed with stars like Quincy Jones, Sonny Rollins, Chet Baker, and Lionel Hampton. The list could go on and on.

Just like local vegetables, local musicians can be the best.

More than Food

WHY DO PEOPLE go out to restaurants? To paraphrase legendary bank robber Willie Sutton, "because that's where the food is." Obviously people look to restaurants and cafes when they want a meal away from home.

Cafes and restaurants also serve a greater function, as revealed by the media attention surrounding the controversy over the habit of some elderly patrons in a Korean neighborhood in Flushing, Queens, who spend large amounts of time in a local McDonald's. Though they are known for fast food, some McDonald's have become a place where the poor, elderly and homeless while away the day, often nursing a single cup of coffee for hours — much to the displeasure of the business owners.

Of course the culture of coffee houses is an old one, and European cafes have a long history of providing shelter and newspapers for their guests. There the idea of asking a patron to leave is anathema to the prevailing mores. Surely there is an element of class involved, because Starbucks has built their business around encouraging patrons to spend time in their stores. Part of the culture of Starbucks is that it is a place where there is free Wi-Fi, and where tech savvy customers can not merely check their email, but actually set up office for the day. Does the discount price of a cup of coffee at McDonald's not entitle customers to the same privilege?

"As long as there have been cities, these are the kinds of places people have met in," said Don Mitchell, professor of urban geography at Syracuse University. In the words of Sango Pak, and elderly Korean gentleman who was a regular at the Flushing McDonalds, "You feel lonely and bored when you are home. Here you talk with friends."

Clearly we go out to restaurants for more than the food. The attacks on the World Trade Center on September 11th occurred on a Tuesday, when Castle Street Café is closed. I wasn't sure whether to re-open the following day, as the country was still in shock, and glued to CNN. We ultimately decided to open, but we didn't expect a very busy day. We were amazed to see the place

Pistachio Cranberry Cookies

Ingredients:

3 cups flour	grated zest of 2 oranges
1 t cinnamon	1 cup shelled pistachios
½ t salt	⅔ cup dried cranberries
1½ cups butter	2 eggs, beaten
½ c sugar	coarse sugar

Directions:

1. Beat together butter, sugar, and orange zest, until soft

2. Add flour slowly, in batches, with cinnamon and salt

3. Add pistachios and cranberries

4. Roll dough into logs, using aluminum foil

5. Chill until hard

6. Brush egg over outside of dough, and roll in coarse sugar

7. Slice the logs into medallions, and bake 15 minutes at 350°.

absolutely packed. People needed a place to gather, and be in the presence of others, and the Café functioned as a public square that day. You can cook and eat at home, but if you seek the company of friends, neighbors, and fellow citizens, you may need to dine out.

Although people sometimes complain that restaurants are too noisy, a silent restaurant is far worse than a noisy one. When we go out to a restaurant we often seek out the buzz and excitement of being in a roomful of fellow humans, and we want to feel and hear their presence, look at how others are dressed, and listen in on conversations.

Restaurants serve other functions as well. In recent times it has practically become a crime to need to use a restroom in this country. Many stores and businesses prominently display signs that say restrooms are for patrons only, even though public restrooms are few and far between, including in downtown Great Barrington. Castle Street Café rarely serves lunch, but the front door is often open, particularly in nice weather. I frequently encounter people with a sheepish look on their face, entering the closed restaurant, asking if they might use the restrooms. My answer is always yes, whether they are adults or children. Aside from the simple humanitarian impulse, it doesn't cost me anything, and I figure some may return for dinner someday, especially after they get a good view of the Café. I never eat at fast food restaurants when travelling, but sometimes I take advantage of their facilities, which is the best thing one can do in them, at least from my perspective.

The perfect accompaniment to a cup of coffee is something that can be dunked. It turns a cup of coffee from something to be guzzled on the go, fast food style, into something to linger over while dunking, and chatting with friends. In my family such a thing is referred to as a "with", as in, something enjoyed with a cup of coffee. The following recipe for pistachio cranberry shortbread yields cookies perfect for dunking.

Fiddleitis

T HOSE OF US OLD ENOUGH to remember an age when the world wasn't 24/7/365 can recall a time when dinner out in a nice restaurant meant soft lighting, mood music, candlelight, and flowers. Wait, we still do that! A great deal of thought and energy goes into creating the right mood and ambiance in a restaurant, which is why it is distressing to walk out into a softly lit room and see the glow of little digital devices, and the majority of diners fiddling with small gadgets. Like many other diseases, fiddleitis is very contagious.

Many guests are unable to get through a meal without checking messages, email, or sending texts, to say nothing of trying to conduct business or personal affairs in a crowded dining room. Technology has changed us, intruded into our lives, and taken over in ways we scarcely notice or understand.

We're all only a few generations away from a time when most of us spent the majority of our time picking berries, hauling water, and hunting game. It is not an accident that a generation that has never grown much

of its own food consumes an astounding quantity of fast food and junk food. We are losing the capacity to enjoy a long and slow home cooked meal without distractions and interruptions.

The fascination and preoccupation with technology has infiltrated the kitchen as well. Led by the renowned Spanish chef Ferran Adrià, there is an upcoming generation of chefs who take their inspiration more from the chemistry lab than the farm. They are more interested in manipulating the physical properties of ingredients in novel ways, than in faithfully recreating the cuisine of their culture. Just as I have no interest in getting my body pierced or tattooed, I have no interest in using sophisticated methods to turn my food into gels, foams, or powders, as is the wont of these "molecular deconstructionists."

Few chefs would seriously suggest, as our current Supreme Court Chief Justice does, that there is some hallowed document endowed with "Original Intent" that must be slavishly followed. Times change, and we must change with them. Nouvelle cuisine was in part a revolt against many of the outdated traditions of French cuisine. For one thing, we now know a lot more about the relationship between eating and good health.

The truth is, we don't handle the stress of this technology very well, and evolution has not adapted us to be on call all the time. We humans require rest and repose. Though we may well be approaching a time when humans evolve to have ports or adapters on our bodies so we may more fully integrate with machines, at the moment we do not, and we still have to eat the old fashioned way.

This recipe for Chicken with Cortland Apples is not only the kind of seasonal comfort food that warms the soul as the nights get colder, but it also uses some very traditional ingredients like apples and apple cider. It

Chicken with Cortland Apples and Cider Sauce
(Serves 4)

Ingredients

2 Cortland apples	2 T minced shallots
4 8-10 oz. French breasts of chicken (with the wing joint attached)	Dash nutmeg
	2 cups apple cider
	½ cup heavy cream
	Salt and pepper

Directions

1. Preheat oven to 350°

2. Slice the apples into quarters, remove the core and seeds, and cut into thin slices.

3. In a large skillet, heat a little butter or vegetable oil, and when hot add the chicken skin side down. Season with salt and pepper, and brown for 2-3 minutes.

4. Turn the chicken over, and add the shallots and sliced apples to the pan. Brown for 2 more minutes.

5. Add a dash of nutmeg, then the cider, and cover the skillet with a top. Place in the preheated oven for 5-7 minutes.

6. Remove the skillet from the oven, and take off the top. Place the skillet on top of a burner, and cook for another 2 minutes, until the liquid reduces by almost half.

7. Add the cream, cook for one more minute, and serve.

is my hope that the process of preparing and serving this meal will foster some long slow dinners, free of electronic interference.

The Chef Has No Clothes On

No, THIS ARTICLE is not about chefs preparing food in the buff. Though given the exalted status of celebrity chefs and the pornographic nature of much of what is already on television, it's really not that much of a stretch to imagine a reality TV show with naked chefs. No, this is about the responsibility of diners to let chefs know when they have crossed the line from innovation into absurdity. Restaurateurs and chefs are obliged to graciously serve their customers with well-prepared dishes made from high-quality ingredients. But diners have responsibilities as well. In addition to showing up on time for reservations, and calling to cancel if unable to come, it is incumbent upon patrons of good restaurants to provide feedback about new dishes and the quality of their meals.

I recently had dinner at one of New York City's hottest, most highly rated restaurants, where a relatively young chef has received enormous attention for serving cutting edge cuisine in an unlikely location. wd~50 is named after its chef, Wylie Dufresne, and its location at 50 Clinton Street on the Lower East Side. It has received rave reviews from the likes of *NY Magazine* and the *New York Times*.

As in so many other contemporary art forms in which no objective standards exist, it is hard to define what is innovative and what is nonsense. If I drop a pile of ladles and spatulas on the floor and record the sound, is that a sonata for kitchen utensils? Can an arrangement of dirty sauté pans and knives on a gallery or museum floor be regarded as a piece of installation art? Similarly, can any outrageous combination of ingredients be considered cuisine?

Like Star Trek adventurers who boldly explore where no one has been before, contemporary chefs are pushing the edge, sometimes successfully, other times not. A hallmark of Chef Dufresne's menu is the listing of ingredients, presumably in the order of their importance to the dish. I started with a dish of foie gras with watermelon, pistachio, sea bean, and lovage. Watermelon is very much in vogue at the moment, and foie gras is traditionally served with various kinds of fruit, so this was not a big culinary leap. There was perhaps a single finely minced pistachio on the plate, enough to detect for a brief, fleeting moment. The other listed ingredients were also used in such small quantity as to hardly matter.

This raises the subject of portions. It has long been true in restaurants that the higher the menu price, the smaller the portion. No one would suggest that quantity is the standard by which cuisine should be judged, or that Americans—already the most obese people in the world—should eat more. Many restaurants serve obscenely large portions of steak and pasta, far in excess of what is necessary or healthy for diners. But when a listed ingredient in a dish is served in such exceedingly small quantity, it scarcely has any impact on the dish. Some of the sauces on Chef Dufresne's plates must have been applied with a tiny eyedropper. When a droplet of sauce about the size of an "o" on this page is put on a plate, it is barely even a garnish, let alone a sauce.

Next, the entrée: turbot served with salsify, smoked bulgur, and coffee saffron was a mixed experiment. The portion of fish, about the size of my thumb, was moist, but tiny. The salsify was raw and unchewable. I normally like virtually all smoked food, including various cheeses and fish, but the bulgur was unidentifiable and unpleasantly gritty. The coffee sauce was the one interesting aspect of the dish worth further exploration, though the coffee was so strong there was no hint of the saffron.

Dessert was the most naked course of the whole meal. Soft chocolate, avocado, licorice, and lime tasted every bit as weird as it sounds. Why not serve chocolate with linguine, octopus, and horseradish? I am normally fond of chocolate in most of its forms, and it takes some effort to render it unappealing. Chocolate shares an affinity with a wide range of ingredients like hazelnuts and almonds, cherries, raspberries, bananas, and oranges, not to mention whipped cream. The lime in the dish is closest to making sense, but the avocado and licorice were truly bizarre.

Just as few want to argue that only representational art is true art, or that only tonal music is legitimate, I am hardly suggesting that we stick to eating the tried and true classics. Eating would be pretty boring if we only ate meatloaf and mashed potatoes or stewed chicken, though each is perfectly delicious and I serve both in my restaurant. Nothing has changed food more around the world than the cross-cultural importing of techniques and ingredients unimaginable just a generation ago. Thirty years ago in this country, Chinese food meant mostly sweet and bland Cantonese cuisine, sushi was a rarity, cheese was Velveeta, and lettuce was iceberg.

Many of the dishes and ingredients we now accept as commonplace are the result of innovation and experimentation, and the forging of new culinary paths. The food processor alone has had an enormous impact on cooking, enabling chefs to puree and process ingredients in ways they had not before. Widespread availability of ingredients like ginger, lemongrass, kiwis, as well as fish and produce flown halfway around the world—and the ways these ingredients are now combined—has fundamentally changed modern cuisine.

The food at wd~50 is constructed, or perhaps deconstructed, according to some abstract theory, sort of like twelve-tone music. It is serious, thoughtful food, prepared by very skilled chefs, and made with high quality ingredients. It just doesn't taste good, and I found the food profoundly soulless. Nonetheless, many leading food critics have been conned into hyping this as the next new trend.

We're most assuredly not in Kansas anymore when dining on this food. While I don't hold up turn of the century Kansas as my ideal in cuisine, I'm not afraid to let the chef know when he doesn't have any clothes on. I trust the reader will have the same courage when they next encounter a naked chef.

Familiarity Breeds Content

RARELY HAS ANYONE written as well about restaurants, and what they can mean to us, as Frank Bruni did in an article recently published in the *New York Times*. To my knowledge, Mr. Bruni, former *NY Times* restaurant critic, has never dined at Castle Street Café. Even so, I felt like he was describing the Café, and the spirit behind it with unusual accuracy. Titled "Familiarity Breeds Content," Bruni sings the praises of those restaurants that keep on drawing him back. "What you have with a restaurant that you visit once or twice is a transaction. What you have with a restaurant that you visit over and over is a relationship."

He characterized his former life as a restaurant critic as "a paid philanderer," exhausting, and constantly on the prowl for the latest trendy place. He recalled his earlier life in Rome and the cafés he liked to eat at while there. Bruni wrote, "The servers and owners there would exult when I walked through the door, because they understood how to make me happy and they could have a conversation with me different from the ones they had with newcomers, a conversation built on shared history and reciprocal trust, a dialogue between honest-to-goodness friends. I wasn't special. But I was special to them."

Of course during the summer and foliage seasons many area restaurants are busy serving tourists and out of town visitors, but the plain truth is that restaurants rely on regular customers. I often joke with regulars that I don't need a doctor's note to excuse an absence, as customers start to explain that illness or out of town weddings were the reason we haven't seen them recently. We have one elderly gentleman who always comes to dine early on Mondays every week, and when he didn't

appear at his normal appointed time, we called his house just to make sure he was all right. That's when you know you are a regular.

I spend most of my time in the kitchen rather than the dining room, and so I rely on my host staff and bartenders to know not just the preferences of my regular customers, but to know their parents' and children's names. Diners can be amazingly territorial about where they like to sit, and when you are a regular, you are more likely to have your seating request honored. When you are a regular, the bartender starts to make your favorite drink before you even sit down. And yes, some steaks are better than others, and when you are a regular, you're more likely to get one of those.

Just as importantly, Bruni wrote, the affection customers feel for a restaurant changes the nature of the relationship. As one of his favorite NYC restaurateurs observed, "It has such a huge impact on the morale of the staff, to see people falling in love with what you're doing. The diner who comes back again and again is a validation, a vindication."

As he aptly observed, dining out can be a stressful experience. What's the best item on the menu? Is it better to sit in one room rather than another? Where is it likely to be quietest? Will the kitchen honor my special request to add or delete an ingredient from a dish? Will I be able to make a last minute reservation on a busy night? When you are a regular, all these questions and issues are addressed easily.

One way a restaurant can cultivate regulars is to have a fairly-priced wine list. Customers aren't stupid, and they have some idea what wine costs. No one wants to feel like they are being taken advantage of by unjustifiably high prices on a wine list. Price the bottles fairly, and diners will come back again and again, knowing

Sautéed Shrimp with Saffron Risotto Cake (Serves 4)

Risotto with Saffron and Shrimp is an old standby in many Italian restaurants. The following recipe, in which the risotto is made into cakes is, is just different enough to be slightly surprising, yet at the same time familiar enough to be comforting.

Ingredients:

24 peeled and deveined shrimp

vegetable or olive oil

1 T minced shallot

1 red pepper, diced

1 cup blanched broccoli florets

½ t minced garlic

1 t finely chopped basil

½ cup dry white wine

2 T soft butter

6 small risotto cakes (see recipe)

Directions:

1. Heat the oil in a large skillet and, when hot, add the shrimp. Cook for 1 minute, then turn over and add the minced shallots and red pepper.

2. Cook for one minute, then add the broccoli, garlic, basil and white wine.

3. Allow the wine to reduce, turn off the flame, and swirl in the soft butter.

4. Remove the risotto cakes from the oven, place one in the center of each plate, divide the shrimp and sauce among the plates, and serve immediately.

they are getting good value for their money.

And then of course there are people's favorite dishes. A huge number of diners know exactly what they want to eat before they get here, without looking at the menu.

Saffron Risotto Cakes

(Yields 6 small risotto cakes)

Ingredients:

1 cup Arborio rice	5 cups chicken stock
1 T minced shallot	3 T grated Parmesan cheese
Pinch saffron	1 T butter

Directions:

Preheat oven to 350°

1. In a heavy bottomed sauce pot, lightly sweat the shallots until translucent, and then add the rice and saffron.

2. After one minute, slowly add a little of the stock, just enough to cover the rice with liquid.

3. Use a wooden spoon to stir the rice, and slowly add just one cup of stock at a time.

4. The rice will require about 20 minutes of gentle simmering.

5. After 20 minutes, remove the pot from the stove, add the butter and cheese, and stir well.

6. Remove the cooked risotto onto a flat sheet pan, so it can cool.

7. When cool enough to touch, form the rice into small cakes, about 2" wide, and 1-1½" thick.

8. When ready to serve, butter a metal baking dish and place the risotto cakes in a 350° oven for 10 minutes, then turn over and cook another 5 minutes. They should be nicely browned, slightly crispy on the outside, and soft and chewy in the middle.

Solace and familiarity are what many people look for when they go out to eat. They have memories of garlicky steamed mussels, grilled Cornish game hen, or thinly sliced calf's liver with caramelized onions, and other dishes they never make at home.

You know you have really made it when a restaurant names a dish after you. For years we served a chicken breast stuffed with spinach and portabella mushrooms, which was a favorite of some very regular and long-standing customers. Of course we change the menu from time to time, and at some point we introduced a different chicken dish. This couple preferred the earlier dish, and I explained that I would be happy to make it for them, and that all they had to do was ask. Further, if they called even half an hour in advance of their arrival, it would make it easier to accommodate their request. They started doing exactly that, and we now refer to the dish as Chicken Marvin, in their honor.

There will always be new culinary trends, be it foams, gels, or fusion cuisines, and there are those who like culinary surprises. But there will also always be a place for those familiar dishes we know and love, exactly because we know and are comforted by them, served by a familiar waiter in a favorite place, as in the following recipe for Sautéed Shrimp with Saffron Risotto Cake. *Bon Appétit!*

PART VI

In Memoriam

· ·

Over the course of 25 years,
we have met a lot of people and made a lot of friends.
Sadly, we have also lost some friends.

Al Schwartz 1946-2011

WHEN ONE FIRST APPROACHES the Castle Street Café, the first noticeable thing is that the Cafe is located immediately next door to the Mahaiwe Theatre. Originally founded in 1905 as a Vaudeville theatre, it has since operated as a movie theatre, and it is now a performing arts center. For over a century, the Mahaiwe has been a beloved part of Great Barrington; but when I first considered buying the Café, its future was very much in doubt. A foreign movie theatre chain had acquired the Mahaiwe in a corporate buyout, and the Mahaiwe was the only single-screen theatre they operated. They planned to convert the historic theatre into a modern multiplex. Many, including me, were concerned that the Mahaiwe would close. But not on Al's watch.

Over a thirty-year career as General Manager of the Mahaiwe, Al Schwartz not only kept the theatre alive but also thriving. When he first took over the theatre in the mid 70's it was closed weekdays and showed porno movies on the weekend. Under his stewardship, the Mahaiwe consistently showed the best Hollywood and independent-art movies, which was a boon to the Café. In addition to screening movies, the theatre hosted film festivals as well as live concerts by artists like Bonnie Raitt, Marvin Hamlisch, and Arlo Guthrie.

Like lots of other people, I think I first met Al as he stood outside the theatre under the marquee, push broom in hand, sweeping the sidewalk. No job was too small for him. Al liked to survey his domain, and the Mahaiwe was definitely his territory. Whether you were a titan of Wall Street or the local plumber, everyone was heartily and equally welcomed to the theatre by Al.

Restaurants and theatres share in a symbiotic relationship. Every night the curtain goes up and patrons come out — many to dine in a restaurant before the show. We rejoiced in sharing this relationship and in having a neighbor who also worked long hours, lived a similar night lifestyle, and obviously enjoyed his work.

Famed film critic Pauline Kael was a Great Barrington resident in her later years, and film studios would arrange to have her preview a movie yet to be released. Those screenings would take place after the regular programmed movie at the Mahaiwe, around 9 or 9:30. That was just as we were finishing up at the Café, and it was a real treat to see a movie preview.

For many years we formed a partnership, Castle Street Productions, which consisted mostly of evenings of foreign films, with the matching ethnic cuisine at the Café. Those evenings helped bring out guests for both dinner and a movie.

At the end of *Casablanca*, as they walk away arm in arm, Humphrey Bogart turns to Claude Rains and says, "Louis, I think this is the beginning of a beautiful friendship." And so it was for many years.

Tom McCain 1938-2010

TOM AND HIS WIFE WENDY began eating at the Café during our first year or so of business, and I got to know them as regular diners. One night, Tom told me that he was studying at the French Culinary Institute in New York. After that, I'd stop by their table to say hello, and Tom would mention what he was learning in school and what he had made that day.

I couldn't have been more surprised when Tom asked if I needed any help in the kitchen. He told me that he would be completing his course work in the spring and would be up in the Berkshires for the summer. My surprise came from the fact that at the time Tom was in his 50's, almost old enough to be my father, and still owned a seat on the New York Stock Exchange. I gathered that Black Monday and the Wall Street crash of October 1987 had been a painful and unpleasant experience for Tom, so he decided to make a major life change.

I thought Tom was joking at first, but it became apparent over time that he was absolutely serious. Tom had already had a long career in the business world that he really didn't like much, and it was clear he had a real passion for food. I figured I didn't have much to lose. He had a pretty good idea that the rate of compensation at Castle Street was quite a bit different than on Wall Street, but we quickly agreed on salary. Tom could have easily retired and spent his time on the golf course,

but he loved cooking and was ready to take on a new adventure. We came from very different backgrounds and work experiences, but we respected and admired the choices we made and the paths that led each of us to work at Castle Street Café. We both had been attracted to the allure of life in the Berkshires.

To say working in the kitchen of Castle Street was a change of pace from his previous work is the understatement of the century. Tom took his responsibilities very seriously and justifiably, and had a lot of pride in his work. He rolled up his sleeves and got sweaty and dirty like the rest of us. He made a mean Pear Tart Tatin that became a signature dessert and was very much part of the early years of the Café.

Einar Aas 1934-2008

FOR ALMOST TWO DECADES, from November through March, after the local ski area closed for the day, we could always count on Einar Aas and his merry band of Ski Butternut instructors to stop in to warm up over a Rob Roy or his favorite glass of "shitty red wine." Einar was not one for pretense. He grabbed the gusto in life and was such an enthusiastic, fun guy to be around that other people gravitated to him. He was one of those men who attracted a crowd wherever he went, and you knew you were going to have a good time just being in his presence. Einar, emissary from Norway, embodied the spirit of Ski Butternut. He was the Life of the Party and Leader of the Pack, loyal and devoted friend, and mascot of Castle Street Café.

In over 30 years in the food business, he is the only person for whom I catered both a wedding and a funeral. Einar remarried later in life, and the Café was the site of a joyous celebration, the place where he and his bride had been coming for many years. When they married, Einar had already had a bout with cancer, but that didn't dissuade Nancy from marrying him even though she had lost her first husband to cancer at a tragically early age. Ten years after they married, Einar's cancer reappeared and he valiantly battled the cancer for more years than anyone ever should, and he did so with an aplomb and grace I envy.

The evening after calling hours at the funeral home, many of his friends assembled at the Café, knowing that he too would have headed there if he could. It's not the only way to measure a man's life, but the throngs that waited for hours to pay their respects at his wake is one indication of the widespread love and affection people felt for him.

His memorial service, held at the ski area, was standing room only, with hundreds in attendance. He had been quite the lady's man before marrying Nancy, and at the memorial service, his best buddy asked the crowd a question that brought some comic relief: "You don't need to raise your hand, but how many of you have slept with Einar?" After the crowd stopped laughing, he continued, "Well, I have slept with Einar lots of times, sharing a room on many skip trips, and I never knew anybody who had to get up and go to the bathroom so many times at night!" Alas, that was the early sign of the cancer that would eventually take his life.

We often joked about *lutefisk*, the traditional and pungent fish dish native to Norway, but of course I never made it. Einar's own unique contribution to gastronomy was his invention of putting M&M's in chicken soup, a dish that few others could imagine.

Toward the end, weakened by radiation, chemotherapy, and the onslaught of disease, he had difficulty eating and had lost the kind of weight that is profoundly disturbing to witness. But he could still eat soup, and it was one of the few foods he desired and was capable of eating. Norwegian that he was, he loved rich creamy fish chowder, with his beloved red potatoes. Just days before he died, I brought him some of this soup. Those of us still living make this recipe in his fond memory.

Einar's Fish Chowder
(Serves 6-8)

Ingredients

1 Spanish onion, peeled and sliced

2 carrots, diced

⅓ head of celery, diced

2 T flour

4 cups fish stock

8 small red potatoes, cut into chunks

⅓ lb. sea scallops

8 oz. salmon, cut into pieces

8 oz. cod, cut into pieces

4 cups heavy cream

Salt and pepper

Splash of sherry

Chopped parsley or dill

Directions

In a heavy-bottomed saucepot, lightly brown the onions. Add the carrots and celery.

Add the flour and stir well, making sure there aren't any lumps.

Add the fish stock and mix well. Then add the potatoes, pieces of fish, and cream.

Let simmer about 25 minutes, taste for salt and pepper, and add sherry and parsley just before serving.

Design

Cover design: Ben Hillman

Book design & production: Bill Cooke

Printing: Lightning Press

Photo Credits

Berkshire Food Journal — Pages 11, 14, 15, 64, 71 and all photos on pages 87 thru 105

Stephen G. Donaldson Photography — Page 115

Michael Lavin Flower — Page 16

Ogden Gigli — Pages 20, 23, 30, 48, 50, 52, 54, 63, 67, 69, 73, 77, 126

Lucky 5 Swing Band — Page 123

Kevin Sprague — Page 56

Don Victor — Page 134

Songbird Essentials, backyardchirper.com — Page 29

Paula Begley, thesaucysoutherner.com — Page 34

Igor Yaruta, 123rf.com — Page 43

Yulia Davidovich, 123rf.com — Page 46